SHORT & FUN STORIES

Hi There Reader!

Welcome to the Short & Fun Stories, Vol. 2 anthology, designed for the busy person with a few minutes to escape.

Within these pages are some of the best writers in the business. You will laugh, cry, ponder and shiver, just like with any great novel. The advantage here is that you will get right to the meat of the action, within minutes, without frills.

Unlike other short story collections, this one is by several different authors, thus the *variety* is beyond wonderful, it is awesome!

Among the authors are successful published writers with many prize-winning full-length novels and one or two brand new writers starting out.

Following each story you will find a short bio of the author and an introduction to his/her novels, for your consideration. If you find an author you like, there are easy links to more books by the same writer.

We have done our best to see that the contents are acceptable for G (General) and GP (General with parental guidance) readers.

Mercer Pub & Friends

ISBN 13: 978-1-97562-945-8
ISBN 10: 1-97562-945-0
Publisher: Mercer Publications & Ministries, Inc.
Stanwood, Michigan, USA

TABLE OF CONTENTS

Don't Order the Fish
Doug Maxson

It was the summer of 1970. We were newlyweds, a couple in love, and going fishing for the first time as Mr. and Mrs. As we approached the waterfront at the end of a narrow dusty two-track, a slight breeze carried the smell of lake weeds and fungus bordering the sloped banks. Tied to a wooden dock, a twelve foot metal craft awaited as our floating carriage with a set of weathered oars that powered the boat.

From the trunk of our sea green colored convertible, I took out two fishing poles, a tackle box, and a pair of aqua blue life preserver cushions. As I carried our gear to the boat, I asked Deb, my wife, to bring the cottage cheese container tucked away in the Styrofoam cooler.

She asked, "What's with the cottage cheese?"

"It's not cottage cheese. It's worms," I replied.

Deb dropped the container. The lid popped off which allowed some of the crawlers to find refuge as they separated blades of grass in their escape. She screamed, "The worms are getting away! I can't move! There's one on my shoe!"

As I walked back to the car, I questioned if this fishing trip was a good idea. I picked up the bait container and recovered most of the worms. We made our way to the boat. I helped her take a seat at the front where a life preserver and fishing pole were placed. A cushion and pole was set in the middle seat where the oars were locked. As I looked at Deb, she sat as still as

6

a statue and asked, "Do you think this boat is safe? It looks ...umm ..."

"Old?" I supplied. "As long as it doesn't take on water it's fine," I assured her.

As we positioned ourselves on the canvas preservers, I gripped the frayed rope tied to the dock questioning myself, *I wonder how long it's been since this boat has been in the water?* I untied the boat, unlocked the oars, and began rowing. With each slap of those water sticks, crystal droplets of water danced about our heads. The only thing missing was a serenade.

Approximately fifty yards from shore, I let down the anchor hoping this would be a good spot. I pulled a crawler from the blue and white container and started to thread it onto the hook.

Deb turned her face away and said, "How can you be so insensitive. That has got to hurt."

I thought to myself, *Be careful now*, and said, "Honey. Sweetheart. Think of it as putting spaghetti on a fork. Now you try it."

A pole and line was shoved in my face. "You do it. You bait the hook. I'll catch the fish."

I wrapped a worm around Deb's hook, and again she turned away in disgust. I was the first to cast a line in the water. It took a few tries for her to cast and release her line without crossing mine. We watched a loving duet of red and white bobbers floating together atop a clear motionless lake, rather a simile of our togetherness.

Then, Deb's bobber did a gentle curtsy sending ripples followed by an ecstatic plunge below the water.

"Jerk the line! Set the hook!" I shouted. "Get that fish in the boat, and I'll take you out to dinner." A rather odd proposition, but would it be enough to turn a day of fishing into a candlelight dinner for two?

Deb jerked the line forcing the bobber to surface causing the pole to take a bow. Something was on her line. But something was also at her feet. She screamed, "There's water coming in the boat! Start rowing to shore!"

I knew what the problem was. In her excitement, her foot kicked open the drain plug seated in the bottom of the boat letting water rush in like a flowing well. I said, "Let me come back and fix it."

"No!" she yelled. Instead, she improvised her own fix by inserting one of her fingers into the opening to slow down the flow of water. Fortunately, we didn't have far to reach shore. Deb kept screaming. I kept rowing.

The scraping of metal against a stone bottom was heard from the bow of the boat. We had touched the shoreline. Deb's finger resembled a cork in a champagne bottle still plugging the hole. She looked exhausted, but relieved. I wanted to laugh, but thought, I'd better not. Deb slowly removed her finger from the drain area and said, "Don't say a word."

After I helped her out of the boat, she sat on the bank with no intention of helping me take the fishing gear to the car. She rubbed her finger trying to bring relief to the redness and soreness it endured.

I noticed our fishing lines were still in the water, and reeled mine in first, placing it beside the tackle box. When I started to retrieve her line, the pole bent with resistance, so I knew there was something still on her line. Maybe this day would not be a total loss. As I reeled in the line I anticipated a prized catch such as a pike or bass. Not so.

It was an ugly whiskered black-faced bullhead from the catfish family. (Sorry God.) He really is a hideous creature. It was obvious Charley was not going home with us. Though ugly, he still deserved a name.

I could see the gold hook deep in Charley's mouth. Bullheads have a tendency to swallow the hook. I took my long needle-nose pliers from the tackle box and started to remove the hook.

Deb said, "I'm going back to the car. I can't watch you rip his throat out."

"His name is Charlie."

"I don't care if his name is Prince Charles. I'll see you at the car."

It was obvious Deb had seen enough of this place and fishing. I picked up the fishing gear, walked to the car and put it in the trunk. When I got in and sat next to her she asked, "What did you do with the fish?"

"I let him go. I'm sorry this day didn't go well. But you know what honey, we are still going out for dinner."

Deb took my hand, smiled and said, "Just don't order the fish."

Walking Tall

Doug Maxson

Arnie Maxson

As I walked down the painted concrete steps to my parent's basement, the tools of the woodworker lay on work tables without their craftsman. Dad was gone now. Sanders, drills, hammers, and saws carried a blanket of dust. The shelves were still lined with mason jars. Inside were assorted nuts, bolts, and screws. Attached to a floor joist above was a carousel of jars with washers, small nails, and miscellaneous hardware that could be rotated by hand, which was one of my father's creations.

His masterpiece was in the corner next to the band saw. Two wooden sticks with work shoes attached to the bottom, draped with old faded curtains, would no

10

longer be strapped to my dad's feet. And what were these? Homemade stilts. They made their debut in 1958 in which I was eight years old, and would become my father's showpiece for the next ten years.

The stilts were not his only creation; a character was born. Dad's wide shoulders donned a black long-tailed coat with a matching black top hat that graced his gray thinning hair. Pinned to the lapel was a sheriff's badge, a rather tarnished piece of silver, yet it had a certain radiance. Behind black-rimmed glasses and a big red nose, a gentle smile prevalent with each step caused those curtain covered stilts to unfurl as flags in a gentle breeze.

My father often performed at family reunions. When he put on those extended legs, it was show time! Some laughed. Some cried, especially the little ones. But when his hands reached into those oversized pockets they knew. Those pockets were filled with magic. Dad would toss handfuls of candy in hopes of convincing the children, this tall man was not to be feared.

This family tradition also became a yearly Halloween night event in my hometown of Grand Ledge, Michigan. Dad would drive downtown, park on the street, and strap on his stilts from the top of his green '54' Pontiac. His chosen route was a three block walk down main street. Business owners would shut down and stand among the crowd. Children turned city curbs into front row seats.

Some tried to keep up with my father's long strides, taking ten steps to his one. He would reach into his pocket and toss candy as if it were from a second story window. Kids would run from everywhere snatching it up.

One Halloween, my father had stopped to talk to the manager of the Sun Theatre. Sam had to look up at my dad and asked, "How would you like to help me with a little project? I'll throw in two theatre tickets."

Dad wasn't sure what he was getting at, but said, "Sure Sam, what have you got?"

"I'll be right back Arnie." Everyone called my father Arnie, short for Arnold.

Sam returned with a box of yellow bulbs, the kind you see lighting up a theatre billboard. He said, "Could you please replace the burned out ones? It would save me getting my ladder. Besides, I don't like heights."

"Sure Sam," Dad smiled. "Is it alright if I give the tickets to a couple of the kids?"

"Sure Arnie." Sam still had to get a small step ladder to get the bulbs into my father's hands. What a sight! Flashing cameras captured the moment, pictures that soon appeared on the front page of the local paper.

Dad was like a circus performer, always looking for a new act. He took stilt walking to the next level, converting a three speed bike of mine extending both seat and handlebars to accommodate for riding with stilts. This restructuring was anything but suicidal. Though I loved that bike, I wasn't about to wrestle it from a twelve foot giant. Besides, this was my father. When you love someone as talented and committed to entertaining kids and adults as my dad was, that's priceless.

My father often took the stilts when visiting friends, knowing he might be asked to entertain. These particular friends lived on a farm, and someone challenged him to kick a football. That's right. On stilts! There didn't seem to be much support for this crazy idea. It was never heard of or ever attempted before. But my dad was up to the challenge.

There were two things he needed to make it work. One, his cane which was constructed from wood to support his left leg, while he raised his right one. Two, someone to toss the football with accuracy for his right leg to make contact. Sound easy? Not really. It took several tosses, perfect timing, good balance, and velocity to connect. Connect he did! That football exploded off his right foot as if shot from a cannon. It took a flight pattern any place kicker in the NFL would applaud. In fact, that projectile cleared the barn roof!

My father would continue to strap on those stilts year after year with his trademark clothing and perfect balance, well into his sixties. When he retired that stilt-walking character, Dad left a legacy. It was a memory of my father 'walking tall'. Literally!

About the Author-Douglas Maxson

My first writing endeavor was over forty years ago entering a writer's contest in our local paper. It was sponsored by Palmers Writer's School looking for new and upcoming talent. This was the same establishment Peanut's creator Charles Shultz attended.

It's ironic that the story, "Don't Order the Fish" was the same submission to Short & Fun Stories that was sent to this contest over forty years ago. (It's much better now.)

A little over three years ago, I discovered a writing critique class held in the back room of a Shuler's Book store. After visiting a couple of times, I was hooked and ready to pursue the writing career.

Because I was now retired from the construction field, I was able to spend more time studying and honing my craft. My wife said she always knew the gift of writing was in me by the pieces of poetry I left for her on napkins while dating her.

With the help and support of West Michigan Writer's Group, I have successfully published two short stories for The Good Old Day's magazine. I like to write fiction, non-fiction, poetry, and memoirs. I've been working on a children's book and hope to complete it for my next accomplishment.

Because I am still in the infant stage of creative writing, I am always looking for support and guidance of which my critique class and Mercer Publications & Ministries, Inc. has provided me.

I also want to thank my Lord and Savior for stirring up that gift of writing which has always been in me.

A Man With No Sense of Humour
Lucinda E. Clarke

The old lady woke with a start. In her dream she had left her bed in the middle of the night, struggled into her dressing gown and searched for her slippers pushed under the bed. Quietly she opened the middle drawer on her bedside cabinet and took out the large serrated knife. No one had noticed that afternoon, after they cut the 100th birthday cake into small slices and handed them round, that Vera had slipped the knife down the front of her elasticated stretch pants and wheeled herself back to her room with the prize. She'd not even stopped to sample the lemon gateau topped with fake whipped cream, intent only on hiding the weapon well out of sight. She'd stuffed it under her voluminous underwear where she was sure no one would see it. She was not planning to keep it hidden for long.

The dream continued. She opened her bedroom door peered out and shuffled as fast as she was able along the corridor, past the reception and waiting area and into the wing on the far side of the residence. Counting the doors on the right, she turned the handle and pushed it open. There he was, Rupert, lying on his back and snoring loudly, his wife lying on the opposite side of the double bed fast asleep. Vera padded forward, bent over Rupert and calmly drew the knife across his throat, pressing down hard to ensure she severed his windpipe.

16

She'd had this dream numerous times, and it was just at this point that she woke up. She lay in the darkness worrying about Susie, the youngest and dearest of all her five grandchildren. Not that Susie was a child anymore. She was in her mid thirties and married, but as yet had not presented Vera with a great grandchild.

She allowed her mind to drift back. Was it only a few weeks ago that Susie had come to see her?

"Hello Gran," she greeted, as, after a brief knock, she bounded into the room.

"Ah, Susie my dear. Come, sit, if you have time."

"I'll always have time for you. I'd visit you more often if I could."

Then to Vera's dismay Susie burst into tears and sobbed bitterly.

"What is it my pet?"

"Oh Gran, I was so happy on my wedding day."

"You were a beautiful bride. Everyone said so."

"Yeah, right." Susie took the lace hanky Vera held out to her and pulled her chair closer to the bed. "Remember what the minister said?"

"I recall he thought himself quite a wit. 'He's yours. You've sworn undying love and affection till death or the divorce courts do you part'."

"It was pretty tasteless and sexist too. He was looking right at me when he said it." Susie sniffed and reached for the box of paper tissues on Gran's bedside table. Her lace hanky wasn't up to the job the tears were streaming down her face.

"He then added I had to play my cards right to snare him in the first place and now all I had to do was learn how to keep him."

"One of the most unpleasant of God's ministers I've ever had the misfortune to meet," Gran said.

"No one ever mentioned the after part," Susie whined. "In all the books boy meets girl, and you see bride and groom disappearing into the sunset to live happily ever after. But they don't, do they Gran?"

"Most times no," Vera replied.

"You and Gramps were married for seventy years, you were happy weren't you?"

Vera's eyes glazed as she looked back into her past. "Yes, we were, but only after I learned how to handle him. Men are quite simple creatures; for example they can't do two things at the same time."

"I need some tips then Gran, teach me what you know. My marriage is falling apart and I'm so miserable."

Vera patted her granddaughter on the arm, sighed and leaned back against her pillow.

"I know that the divorce rates are shooting up and that disgusting vicar was right, catching them is the easy bit. Your best ally is humour."

"I don't feel like laughing," Susie's eyes welled up with tears again. "How can I be funny when all I want to do is cry?"

"Let me give you an example. This comes under exaggeration."

"What?"

"Just listen. It's very useful if you are ever in the wrong. Say you've dented his car, you don't own up straight away."

"He'd be so mad at me," Susie squeaked.

"You could try the following. Rush up to him smother him with kisses, offer him his slippers and serve up his favourite meal before you begin your tale of woe. You include the following: 'it was terrible' ... 'you're going to kill me' ... 'don't stop loving me'...'I'll save for ten years to pay you back' ... 'I never meant to ruin the car like that.'

"You see my dear his mind will be racing by now. The car is a total write-off. You've slaughtered several pedestrians, and he's frantically computing how to raise finance for the court case and a new car. When you finally confess you dented the back bumper he'll actually feel relieved."

"That's pretty sneaky Gran. Did you ever ...?"

"Of course darling, time and time again and in seventy years your Granddad never noticed once."

"I can't see how that would've have helped me last week when he forgot my birthday."

"Oh, the birthday reminder is a classic, but you must prepare well in advance, anything up to six months and this works for Christmas as well."

"Go on then Gran, out with it."

"First you need a calendar, a wish list and several blocks of those 'post it' notes, the fluorescent ones are best. You might as well let the whole world know a special event is coming up."

"And then ...?"

"I forgot you also need one of those black pens with the big furry tips. You write 'Guess whose birthday it is in 32, 23, 11, 5, 2 days time."

"OK OK Gran I get the gist."

"That may not be enough. You must add what you want, and be very specific. 'The dress shop on the corner is having a sale and they have a great dress size - add in the right size here - and these days of course you can take a photo with your phone and attach that too."

"And prime the shop assistant as well!"

"Now you're catching on. It's important to know where to put these notes. I suggest the back of the wardrobe door, on his razor, the car steering wheel, his pillow, attached to his dinner plate."

Despite her misery Susie giggled. "You're really quite devious Gran!"

Vera looked shocked. "Not at all, just wise. It's very important to explain to them in simple terms what you want. They'll never notice if you don't give them a big heave in the right direction."

Susie curled up, making herself more comfortable on Gran's bed. "Go on, I can't wait to hear the next one."

"It's the 'no reason' dinner. This works particularly well if he's the suspicious type. Why are you being warm, romantic and friendly? He'll eye the candles, his favourite food and his automatic reaction will be to staple his wallet and wail about the size of the current overdraft. Once a month or so do the candlelight thing, you know, the flowers, his favourite dish, foot massage, the works - for no reason at all!"

"I get it. He'll be waiting for you to ask for ..."

"... Precisely. It works every time. Pour on the perfume, wear a little number you wouldn't be seen dead in outside the front door and treat him like a sheik."

Susie dissolved into fits of laughter. "I never realised Gran, I just didn't, ha ha."

"Most people don't," the old lady smiled. "We old folks are a lot smarter than you young people think we are. It's the result of years of experience."

"Is that it?"

"Goodness no. That's only the tip of the iceberg."

"Don't stop, I want to hear all your tricks Gran. What else is there?"

"Let me think. The reverse suggestion is good too. The idea is to persuade him that all the best ideas are his. For example say you want to go to Mauritius on holiday this year. You tell him what a silly idea that would be. Just because everyone else is queuing around the block to get those cheap tickets - you will have done a little research on that internet thing all you young people use these days. You announce you're not worried about being with the 'in' crowd on the beaches full of topless women frying under a boiling hot sun. How could other people spend so much money just to lie on a beach and swim in the sea, when Little Bogs by the Sea has exactly the same facilities and the caravan park will be so much cheaper?"

By now Susie had tears of laughter rolling down her cheeks. "What do I say then?"

"Nothing. You've planted the seeds, sit back and watch them grow. Indirectly you've peaked his interest, questioned his manhood and assured him he's not in with the A list. Get ready, pet, to be amazed when he hands you the air tickets."

"You are just so clever Gran."

"No, just wise. Want to hear some more?"

"Yes please."

"The public compliment always goes down well. Praise him in front of his mates he'll love you for it. Men need their egos massaged on a daily basis, but be careful not to overdo it."

"I'll remember that Gran," Susie smoothed out a few wrinkles on her skirt, and twirled a loose thread from the counterpane around her finger.

The old lady noted her nervous gestures. She

looked down at her own gnarled hands, covered in liver spots. She leaned forward and placed an arm round her granddaughter's shoulders.

"I've talked for far too long," she said. "I'm tired; I get so sleepy even during the day now."

"Gran what do you expect for ninety-six years old! I think you're brilliant for your age."

Vera smiled. "I don't know if I've helped any, but think about what I've told you today. See if any of it is useful. Just add in the togetherness factor, don't let him stray too far and think he's single again. He plays rugby doesn't he?"

Susie nodded.

"Then get in there and cut the oranges for half time, it's an excellent way of putting the groupies off. Remind him every day how important he is and practice those winks across a crowded room, those knowing 'together' looks. Know what I mean?"

"Yes Gran we used to do all that stuff before we were married. Now ..."

"It doesn't do him any harm to be reminded how much you depend on him. Yes, yes, I know what you're going to say, we're far superior, but they mustn't find that out, not in a marriage even among modern people these days."

Vera leaned back on her pillows and closed her eyes. All that talking had quite worn her out but the nice thing about her daytime snoozes, unlike her nights, was that she never dreamed about killing Rupert.

Over the next few months Susie reported back on how things were going. She'd tried all her Gran's suggestions. Cooked extra special meals, praised her husband in private and public, winked at him until her eyelids ached, and even whipped up miniature frozen orange lollies shaped like rugby balls for half time breaks.

Nothing was working, Susie reported back. He snarled at her 'over the top' excuses for a minor infringement: mocked her attempts to be warm, loving and kind, sniggered at the outfit she'd bought from Victoria's Secret as only fit for a prostitute and complained she'd never learn to cook a decent meal.

Whenever she got the chance Vera observed Susie and her husband with dismay. The interaction between the two of them showed that all was not well.

Things escalated. Susie didn't come and chat to her in her room as frequently and there were often dark bruises on her face, arms and legs. When questioned, Susie brushed them off as accidents, falls, walking into doors and other unbelievable excuses.

Vera's heart ached for her granddaughter who became more and more miserable as the weeks went by. Vera couldn't bear to watch it any longer. She planned her campaign with great care.

When they came round with the library trolley, Vera chose a rather odd collection of books. The librarian raised her eyebrows but said nothing. Vera had always been an avid reader with a wide taste in literature and her odd request raised no flags.

Her next task was to get hold of a pair of rubber gloves. This was easy. The supply cupboard was seldom locked and it wasn't too difficult to slip inside and grab a pair.

Returning to her room, Vera thought about where she could hide them. The care-home cleaners were pretty efficient. They dared not skimp for everyone was scared to death of the man who ran the establishment with military precision and discipline. It was never a good idea to upset him. Do so and you'd be out on your ear the same day.

Vera decided the most sensible place was in the cupboard under the sink in her en-suite bathroom. She could always deny all knowledge if they were discovered. She pushed the gloves well out of sight wedging them between the waste pipe and the wall.

Then Vera's plan was put on hold when she went down with a very bad dose of flu which kept her confined to her bed for days. She fretted as she lay there. She was only a frail old lady who'd led a very ordinary, uneventful life and now she couldn't do even the most basic things without help.

She wasn't the only member of the family to fall ill to the annual flu strain that was flying around the country sending hundreds to their beds. One of her other granddaughters caught a bad dose, and two of her three children were also infected. Susie caught the train to the next county and went to take care of the family.

The care home was buzzing the day Muriel turned one hundred. They had planned a party for her. The bakery down the road produced a huge cake and a local quartet was coming to play golden oldies music, along with a choir from the nearby primary school.

Vera insisted on attending. Hundredth birthdays didn't happen every day she argued. Couldn't they just push her along in a wheelchair for a short while, to watch Muriel cut the cake?

At first her pleas were only met with sad smiles but the doctor came to her rescue and said as long as she sat quietly it was unlikely to affect her recovery.

Privately Vera wondered if they expected her to get better or simply slip away one night into the next life - if there was one. She was still trying to make up her mind on that question.

So Vera was wheeled into the dining room, insisting her chair be parked right next to the cake and although it was a variation to the dream, the cake knife found its way off the table onto the seat of the wheelchair behind Vera. Afraid she might cut herself, once the steel blade was out of sight, she complained of feeling unwell and asked to be taken back to her room.

Lying there that night it occurred to her that being bedridden provided her with the perfect alibi. No one would even think she could get out of bed, latch on to her walker and make it to the far end of the care home.

At first Vera was very shaky on her pins, but she was a determined lady and practised crawling out of bed when the care home staff was elsewhere. Leaning heavily on her walking frame she shuffled round and round her room. They would have been amazed to see her scoot over the carpet even faster than before she fell ill. She continued to act frail and slightly delirious at times. Vera fooled them all.

At last the big night came. After sleeping most of the day, she dragged herself out of bed, struggled into her dressing gown, pushed her feet into her slippers and, leaning on her walker, retrieved the gloves and the knife.

Vera set off across the home to the third door on the right.

The scene was exactly as she had pictured it in her dreams, except for the absence of his wife. Rupert was on his back, splayed across the bed taking up every inch of it and snoring loudly. The manager of the care home, the same man who abused his wife and terrorised both staff and patients lay there without a care in the world.

Vera shuffled forward and studying his torso for a few moments thrust the knife hard under his ribs and up toward his heart. It was harder work than she'd imagined. She leaned on the frame of the walker and applied both hands to the task.

That's what comes of having no sense of humour, Vera thought, after watching her granddaughter jump through hoops to keep her husband Rupert happy.

She shuffled back to her room unseen and crawled back into her own bed knocking *Anatomy for first Year Medical Students* off the bedside table.

The old lady smiled fondly and fell into a dreamless sleep.

~*~*~*~

Please continue on for an excerpt from Lucinda E Clarke's fabulous multi-award-winning novel about her heroine, Amie's Adventures in Africa.

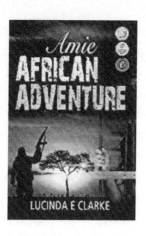

[CLICK HERE for US EDITION](#)
[Click Here for UK edition](#)

(Editor's Note: In the following excerpt, Amie has escaped from jail and is trying to make her way across the African wilderness to safety in a neighboring country.)

Excerpt from:

Amie African Adventure
By Lucinda E Clarke

The next day, she saw a puff adder lying in the sunshine. These were the snakes that did not get out of your way, ignoring the vibrations made by approaching feet. In her hurry to avoid it, Amie ran back several steps and gashed the back of her leg on a sharp thorn bush. She looked in horror as a thin trickle of blood ran down towards her ankle. Now she had two problems. The scent of blood travelled far across the veld, and might attract predators, and there was the danger of infection.

She crept away from the slumbering snake putting a safe distance between them, and sat down to clean the wound and bandage it. Using as much of her precious water as she dared, she dabbed at the area around the scratch as best she could, and then tried to tear off the bottom of her dress to use as a bandage. It looked so easy in the movies, she thought as she tugged and tugged, but the material would not give way. She tried to bite the seams, but only succeeded in hurting her teeth, so in the end she was forced to abandon her efforts and hope the gash would heal quickly.

She began to worry about getting heatstroke. Her legs were cramping more and more frequently, she often felt dizzy and her head ached badly. Her earlier strength was draining away as she doggedly put one foot in front of the other, but all too often, the landscape began to undulate in front of her. She was fearful of losing direction, what if she was not walking towards the border?

She stumbled over to one of the smaller thorn trees and attempted to scramble up into the first fork off the ground, but she simply didn't have the strength to get there. She munched the remaining leaves and took several sips of water. Her supply was running very low and she knew she would have to find more very soon. The shimmering ground looked completely flat in all directions, and there wasn't a dry river bed in sight. She rested up until the sun began to sink in the sky and then forced herself to her knees and using one of the empty water bottles, she dug a shallow hole in the ground. No sign of water at all but maybe she could catch a little dew.

Using a sharp stone, she cut one of the water bottles in half and placed it upright in the bottom of the hole. Over the top, she placed the large piece of plastic she had found at the Lodge, and weighted it down with large stones. Placing one stone carefully in the middle of the plastic directly over the bottle, she could only hope. Thank you Dirk, thank you Dirk for passing on the knowledge, she said to herself over and over and over again.

Exhausted by her labours, she foraged around, and was relieved to see more of the 'safe, succulent, plants' as she thought of them. The ones left in her rucksack had shriveled up and didn't look edible any more. In the cool of the evening, she found the energy to climb a little way up into the tree, dragging the rucksack with her. She was tempted to leave it on the ground, but was afraid an animal might find it and destroy it.

Amie slept fitfully that night, waking every few minutes with cramped arms and legs, or feeling sore where the tree trunk or the bag was digging into her. *I'm getting weaker,* she thought. Several weeks of prison food had not exactly equipped her for long treks, and she knew her spirits were sinking lower and lower. She wasn't sure how much longer she could go on. She had no idea how long she'd been walking, or where she was, or how much farther she had to go. She hadn't thought beyond getting to Ruanga, and she had no idea what sort of reception she might receive there, or how she would get to the capital and contact an embassy or ... *Let me get there first,* she thought, *just let me get there.*

As soon as it was partially light, Amie slid down from the tree and went to examine her homemade still. Lifting the corner of the plastic very carefully, she could see a few drops of water run down the underside towards the waiting bottle. She gave a whoop of joy, but when she'd removed all the plastic, she was dismayed to see there was maybe two tablespoons of water in the bottle. It didn't look particularly clean and it certainly wouldn't be enough to sustain her. Nice idea, Amie, she said to herself, but you will just have to walk for longer and faster each day, rest up for less.

It was a stupid decision.

Even though she knew how hot the sun could get, and what effect it would have on her hydration levels, Amie had underestimated the extent to which it would affect her sense of direction and her will to continue walking.

That day she covered a lot less ground, and with a sense of dread, she sipped the last few drops from the water supply she'd brought with her from the Lodge. She found she was wandering, weaving from side to side, and losing focus on the range of hills which sometimes appeared to be ahead of her, and sometimes to her right or her left.

Her mouth felt dry and her tongue several sizes too large. She ached all over and it was becoming harder and harder to walk. The gash on the back of her leg was throbbing, and she thought it was probably infected. Several times she stumbled. Having lost the energy to step over obstacles, she had trouble focusing, as she tried to weave around the shrubs that sprang suddenly up in front of her.

Her headache got worse and worse and she wanted to vomit, although there was very little in her stomach. She picked some more leaves and squeezed the liquid out of them, catching the meagre amount of sap in her mouth.

But she was not as careful as she had been before, she couldn't concentrate, her vision was fuzzy, and she chose the wrong plants.

About the Author -Lucinda E. Clarke

Abandoned in the African bush with a nine week old baby and no resources Lucinda could look back on a childhood of mental abuse, without knowing that before her lay an even more bizarre future. She would run the worst riding school in the world, broadcast live with a bayonet at her throat, be fired from her teaching position and thrown into the media world. She would learn how to lie in the name of propaganda, write about dozens of topics for a variety of clients and have her own newspaper column. She would meet kings and statesmen, international artists and rural Africans. She would win several awards along the way for her scripting and films. Eventually she would reluctantly leave Africa to retire in Spain. A few months later she would begin writing books - eight to date in a variety of genres - and start a whole new career, collecting more awards.

Back in Europe Lucinda met many people who knew little about Africa except for what they had seen in the media. And so, the *Amie* stories were born, to paint a true picture of the peoples and culture on the Dark Continent wrapped up in a thrilling series of adventures which reflect her love for the lands she unwillingly left behind.

Lucinda writes this about herself:

When it comes to me talking about me and my books I'm a disaster! Do I mention that I've lived in eight countries, in a mansion, a one bed flat and on a boat? I could tell you about running my own video production company, and tales about some of the famous people I've worked with. The problem is there is so much it took three books to put it all down on paper and that's only the bits I remember.

I'm retired now. No, I'm pretending working 24/7 writing books and trying to sell the wretched things. Once I make the first million, or five, I'll be off sailing round the world scribbling on my mega yacht.

I guess I should really mention my books. I'm a multi-genre writer. Since my time writing for radio and television, I've tackled subjects as bizarre as splitting the atom, how to climb a ladder, how a bakery operates, several series on math, English and science, good business practices, how they make potato crisps, programmes for tourism and local and national government and so on and so on and so on. Add in mayoral speeches, adverts, brochures, my newspaper column and magazine articles, and I'm sure you get the message.

So, it was quite a challenge, once I'd scribbled my memoirs, to write a full length novel. I was now my own client. I could write as long or as short as I wanted, set my own deadlines. The freedom was exhilarating. I'd

32

had plenty of those '*clients from hell*' but not one was as bad as me.

I created Amie, who is now so real I'm tempted to lay a place for her at the table. I dragged her unwillingly out of her nice, safe, suburban home outside London and sent her to Africa. Civil war breaks out and she is in real trouble. It is action adventure page-turning stuff in this four book series. Book 4 is due out shortly.

CLICK HERE FOR LUCINDA'S WEB SITE

Or Go Here: https://lucindaeclarkeauthor.com/

Wrestling with Christianity and Bisexuality

Lisa Eskinazi

When I found Christianity in its purest form, I found unconditional love, acceptance and hope. When my sexuality rose to the surface within the pit of my gut, literally seeping out of my skin, wanting to be known, I found confusion, prejudice and a feeling of being lost. So how do the two co- exist?

When I found church, I had reached the bottom of myself. I was bingeing, sleeping erratically and smoking cigarettes until my lung collapsed. I was mentally ill, frequently hospitalized in psychiatric clinics and petrified of being left alone in my flat.

Then... I found God at a local church. I felt a part of something special. I felt worthy. I accepted myself because I was told by kind people that God did too, but then...

I found myself wrestling with my attraction to both sexes. I felt like I couldn't breathe, trapped because I'd finally found what I had been searching for and I was terrified it would be ripped out from under me. And that it would be my undoing.

I attended many churches and received the "Love the sinner but not the sin" line. But the culmination of negative reactions--and I must say the most dangerous thing that can happen and which often occurs to people within the LGBTI community--was when a human being played God. It sent me into a depressive downward spiral.

It happened when I met a lady at a Christian health retreat, she was very set in her beliefs. She was legalistic in her approach and talked about how we should behave, what music we should listen to, what we should eat... You get the picture. The more she pushed, the more I felt I couldn't hide the real me any longer.

She visited me one day at home and I said I had something to tell her. "I'm bisexual." Without a blink of the eye she laid her guitar down next to her chair, clasped her hands together, pursed her lips and said "Your salvation is at stake."

In a place of complete desperation, over many weeks, I began to search for answers. I studied what the Bible said on the topic. But the more I read, the more confused I became. My heart pounded hard in my chest as I began to pour over online articles from pastors arguing their point of view. Each side had good arguments. I was swapping sides of the argument supporting homosexuality to believing it was a sin, continuously and repeatedly changing my opinion, sometimes from one article to the next over several nervous weeks. I felt squashed down yet relentless in my search for the truth. I prayed, read and talked to Christian friends.

Could I be with the girl with whom I had fallen in love and go to hell? Or would I live in hell for the rest of my life without her and be rewarded in heaven?

I was alone. Condemned. And scared for my salvation.

Finally, I came to a simple realization. One that sat calmly within my heart and within my spirit. A quiet knowing, feeling of wisdom. I abandoned the books, articles and countless opinions.

God is love. I am loved. I love her. And I've chosen to live by that insight for the sake of my sanity. Like a tree blowing in the wind I sway from side to side in life's storms but my foundation is rooted in God's love and He is my rock. No more debates, sleepless nights and research over cold coffee, wondering where my destiny lies. I'm a Christian in a lesbian relationship and I love God with all my heart. I don't parade my sexuality around for all to see, nor do I hide it away. But I've learnt to tell people who will understand so as not to stir up debate and uneasiness which may cause unnecessary suffering. It is my choice whom I tell.

I've found love, in God in heaven and I've found love on earth. I think I'm one lucky chick!

Asylum

An Interview by Lisa Eskinazi

Every bone in my body told me I had to share my interview with a Manus Island detainee. It is the right thing to do. He wishes to remain anonymous for safety reasons. His story breaks my heart...

Can you please tell me about where you are from and what the conditions were like?

"I lived in a society where culture is more important than humanity, where open minded people can't speak up , where lips are sewed, where the system has been made by just men, where women are considered to be slaves, where education is not common for girls, where love is a crime, where the punishment of sex is death in public. Unfortunately I was part of that society where I faced unacceptable things, I was told by society to protect the same culture to death and give the same lesson to the next generation. If any one ever tried to go against the society they would be killed and the sad news is more than 90% of the people feel proud to follow the same culture which was made centuries ago."

What led you to have to seek asylum?

"I was trying to speak up for the rights of women and girls but my own family members turned against me and warned me, 'If you go against the culture you will be a dead man.' The fact is I can't fight with 90% of the people of society. My voice and ideas could not change thier minds. I was told 'If you want to survive you have to shut your mouth'.

37

"One day I saw a girl and she was one of the most beautiful girls I have ever seen. I forgot everything, my heart was so happy. Those were such beautiful days. I couldn't propose to her openly (that's not common in our culture) So I asked my cousin's sister to please pass my message to her. My message was delivered to her and she responded 'I really want to meet you.'

"She was a good friend of my cousin and she was coming to my cousin's house sometimes where we would meet secretly. We got to know each other very well and we both were so happy. I promised her 'I will make you happy forever'."

WHAT HE TOLD ME NEXT WAS SHOCKING.

"She is no more! She was killed by her own father because we were caught. I was shocked and did not know what to do. My cousin suggested that I had to leave now.

"Friend's and family turned against me and I received many many phone calls by her family members and they said 'You bring a lot of shame on our faces. We already killed the girl and your death will be a proud moment for our family. You are dead man.' I was hiding in a friend's house and I received a call from my mom and she was crying and telling me 'Please don't come home. People have come to our house and they fired in the air and they are looking for you.' So my friend arranged everything for me to seek asylum in a safe place.

"I broke my promise and I couldn't protect her like she dreamed I would. I failed."

How did you arrive?

"A smuggler promised me that he would send me somewhere safe. But he lied to me. I was detained in the smuggler's cage for two months. I took a lot of risks and I was lucky to finally reach Christmas Island by a risky and leaky boat. When I saw Christmas Island I thought I had finally found safety, but actually I was wrong "

What is your experience of being in detention?

"My life has ended in detention. I have been detained here for the last four years. I was brought to offshore detention by force, against my will. The Australian government changed the policy to not resettle refugees who arrived by boat after the 19th of July 2013 They separated asylum seekers and sent them to Nauru and to the Manus Island Detention Centre. Some of us remain on Christmas Island and later the people who were detained in Christmas Island were released in Australia.

"When I was sent here I was told 'You don't have any rights to say anything. You should go back to your home country otherwise you will be detained here for good, and that's policy.' We wait in the queue for hours for meals in the sun and the place is overloaded. We were locked up in four different compounds where we were not allowed to see each other. The policy was completely tough. Our hopes were taken away, our dreams were taken away. The G4S security treat us like criminals. I heard since my childhood the western countries do respect humanity and give rights to humanity.

"The people were tired of this bullshit and they started to protest in the detention centre in the beginning of 2014 saying 'FREEDOM FREEDOM FREEDOM.' The protest lasted a couple of days but the Australian government didn't care about us. One day it was night when the PNG police--PNG local security including some Australian security--came with weapons and fired bullets into the air to stop the protest. They killed one my friends and left more than seventy injured that was the horrible night. After the incident the government cancelled the license of G4S security and made a deal with a new company called "Transfield" and until today they are running the centre. After the incident people were tense and we were scared of the locals. Time was passing and we were hoping for a positive outcome from the Australian government. Nothing happened and nothing changed.

"In the the beginning of 2015 when we started a hunger strike for our rights we didn't eat anything for two weeks. Many people were sent to hospitals for treatment. The lawyers were fighting for our rights and finally on April 2016 the Supreme Court of Papua, New Guinea declared the Manus Island Detention Centre illegal and ordered both Australian and Papua New Guinea governments to take the urgent step of closing the centre and to release all the innocent men to a safe place.

"Just recently on Good Friday one Navy officer and a refugee began to fight. Many Navy officers started to fire and hit the accommodation and were trying to kill us.

"I don't know what my crime is and I don't know what will happen next. In simple words I can describe this is not a processing centre, this is torture.

"My only crime was to fall in love, and to seek asylum."

This man's story sends a powerful message. I believe in years to come, there will be enquires into our politicians' behaviour, about how they could do this to innocent victims. And there will be apologies, but it will be too late for some.

Fork in the Road

Lisa Eskinazi

(When I was a teenager and I became overwhelmed I would go to the beach and sit on the sand and stare at the waves. On this day I took a walk. And, I made a decision. I believe God helped me make it. I write this poem today because of that decision.)

Fork In The Road

Sea shells. Worn
Down on the tickling edge of foam
Pearl like
She picked up one
Strong, precious
And she placed it back in it's home

The waves poked at her feet
At the sand
At her heart
The water teasing her red painted toenails

Silent trudges
One foot in front of another
Sinking intermittently
It has come to this
Keep walking
Or stop

As sure as the water laps the sand
And her heart beats
She must continue to walk

So she does

About the Author--Lisa Eskinazi

Freelance Writer

I call Melbourne, Australia home where I live to write poetry and non-fiction. Writing for me is both therapeutic and fulfilling of my passion of highlighting social injustices. My aim is also to ignite hope in others who are battling such things as refugee rights, gay rights, putting a stop to bullying and creating awareness and hope around mental health.

A soul/blues/rhythm and blues music addict and a Home and Away fan, I love escaping into a book--my favourites being biographies, thrillers and suspense. I'm a cat person. Another one of my joys is long weird, wonderful and in-depth conversations with those close to me, over a cappuccino.

Singing is a dream to explore someday, but right now, curling up on the couch with my laptop late into the night is just fine and quite enough for me.

My Author Page:

http://web.facebook.com/iwrite4rights?_rdc=IG_rdr

Purchase: "Out of The Well" My Battle with School Bullying and Severe Depression:

http://www.melbournebooks.com.au/products?term=out+of+the+well

The Phenomena

Wareeze Woodson

Sara Beth slowly twisted the glass knob and pushed the door inward listening for the squeak of the hinges. Barely inside the room, a strange awareness overwhelmed her, breathless and disturbing like in her nightmares. In all of her five years on this earth, after such an occurrence, some incident always happened. Being in her own home with the shiny oak floors and big rooms had nothing to do with the sensations. It made no difference. The impressions came anytime, anywhere. Sometimes whatever occurred didn't become apparent until a much later date. She wasn't likely to understand today—maybe not for years to come. Shrugging, she pushed the impression aside.

Sara Beth and Gail

Quietly shutting the troublesome door, she leaned against the wooden panel with her hands behind her back. Gazing around the room at the ivory wallpaper, she sighed and took a quick breath. Yes! She was alone in her mama's bedroom. Course it belonged to her daddy, too, but that had nothing to do with anything.

Hadn't her mama always told her to use her imagination? That's what she intended to do today. Just like the dancer in her grandma's music box, she twirled around and around, her arms extended, her pink skirt billowing out with her movements. Sinking to the floor to stop the dizzy spinning of her head, she inspected the shiny wooden bed with its four posters rising up and up way above her. She liked the silky, lavender bedspread, soft and smooth under her fingertips. Not that she touched the coverlet, but one day, she had allowed her hand to accidently on purpose slide across one corner.

Light streamed in the two long windows through the lace curtains and sparked in the shimmering reflective glass above the vanity. She loved that huge mirror. She could view her entire length in it if she stood on the vanity stool.

Climbing up on the bench, she plopped down on the padded cushion and traced the pattern of roses across the top of the vanity with one finger. This place smelled like her mama, sweet talcum powder, body lotion, and sachet in a little pouch.

Opening the top drawer in the middle, she caught her breath with excitement. She'd found her mama's bobby-pins and imagined herself all grown up, her hair curled, dressed in a fancy dancing gown. She gazed at her reflection staring back at her with big brown eyes, rosy cheeks, and brown hair brushing against her neck.

Her hair didn't suit her, so she divided the locks into sections, lifting a few strains and curling the hair around one finger. She pushed the curl to her scalp and pinned it in place with a bobby-pin just like her mama did. Laboriously, she twisted another curl, then another. Finally finished rolling her entire head of hair, she delved further into her mama's vanity.

She opened another drawer, storage for her mama's jewelry collection. At the center, a gold locket in the shape of a heart inlaid with several rubies sparkled even in the dim light afforded deep in the drawer. Not daring to pick up the necklace, she allowed her fingertip to caress the stones, cool, alluring, and forbidden.

Tires crunched in the gravel drive at the side of the house. Sara Beth slammed the drawer shut and jumped down. She streaked to the living-room in mind of her mama's warning to never open the door to a stranger. She was alone in the house. Her mama went shopping and intended to pick up her older sister from school, but her daddy should be out in the workshop.

She scooted past the deep burgundy sofa, the stuffed armchair, the stone fireplace and the piano to peek outside. The wooden door stood open to let in a soft breeze, but the screen with the iron scrollwork was latched.

She viewed a tall man, his shadow steadily creeping towards her with his every heavy step until it swallowed her up. With his back to the sun, bright light outlined his lanky frame and shaded his features.

Wanting to scream, to run, to escape, she stood rooted to the spot, helpless. He was a grownup, not to be trusted, a stranger as best she could tell. She didn't recognize this man wearing rumpled jeans and a baggy shirt. With his red nose and eyes fresh from weeping, he fisted his hands, opened and then shut his fingers again. He turned away before whirling back, still standing on the concrete porch with the white pillars holding up the roof. He studied her for endless minutes.

Finally, he spoke his voice deep and muffled, "Is your daddy home?"

Sara Beth grinned. She knew that voice. He was Clutch—Mr. Clutch. She struggled to loosen the latch until it popped opened. The screen door creaked at the joints when she pushed on it. "Hi, Mr. Clutch."

A booming laugh sounded behind her. She twirled around. Her daddy, Mr. Travis Dayton, stood in the archway between the living and dining rooms.

Travis moved forward and pulled Sara Beth to his side. "He's not Mr. Clutch. Clutch is his nickname."

Travis stretched out his hand. "Welcome Joe. I heard your truck in the drive."

Joe shook his hand. "I need to talk to you." He stuffed his hands in his pockets leaning back on the heels of his tennis shoes. "I got something to tell you. It's important." He shuffled his feet and glanced at Sara Beth.

Sara Beth sensed this was the time to melt into the background. She wouldn't go play, even though her daddy pointed her in the direction of the archway and patted her back. Moving slowly forward on her way out of the opening, she quickly slipped behind the over-stuffed chair by the fireplace. Crouching, ever so quiet, still as a mouse, and on the alert to every word uttered by the grown-ups, she listened, her favorite thing to do—besides searching around in her mother's belongings.

"Sit yourself down and let's talk," Travis invited.

She paid close attention to Joe's words so she could understand what he said. Mama had told her his voice sounded so muffled because he had a cleft palate—a hole at the back of his mouth. Sara Beth couldn't see a hole, but he did have a funny-looking lip all snarled up in the middle. She could see it through his mustache even from her hiding place.

Joe sank into a chair and propped his elbows on his knees. He dropped his head in his hands, his shoulders shaking. Finally, he wiped his eyes with the back of his hand. "I'm in bad trouble."

"Let's hear it then." Travis settled back in his chair, his long legs stretched out before him and crossed at the ankles.

Joe swallowed. Sara Beth could tell. When she peeked around the edge of the chair, his Adam's-apple bobbed up and down before he spoke.

"Me and some buddies went camping at Galveston. We pitched our tents on the beach way out so we wouldn't disturb nobody. We partied all week, swimming, picnicking, and howling at the moon."

Sara Beth blinked her eyes in disbelief. Only a coyote howled at the moon, not people. She didn't understand, but she knew about partying. She went to a birthday party once. How long was a whole week anyway?

Joe made a funny sound in his throat, like a groan. "A couple of the guys brought some wild women. I brought one to the party as well."

Sara Beth's imagination worked overtime trying to picture a wild woman. Later, she'd ask her daddy if he knew any wild women. She wanted to see one. Joe stopped talking and she peered at him until he started again.

"We didn't do much sleeping, but plenty of drinking, and carousing all night. Some in the day too. The drinking I mean." Joe rolled his eyes, and his restless gaze darted around the room.

Sara Beth ducked completely behind the chair again and covered her legs with her pink skirt. Wrapping her arms around her knees drawn up to her chest, she didn't move except to take a few shallow breaths. She heard his feet hit the floor with a thump. Cautiously, she peeked around the edge of the overstuffed chair.

Joe paced across her mama's best carpet, the big one with the roses on the border. Back and forth, back and forth, his hands in his pockets again.

Halting and with tears running down his cheeks, Joe stammered, his voice pitched higher, "When I woke up this morning, she was dead."

Chapter 2

Sara Beth held back a gasp. She knew what dead meant. Her granny had died and went to Heaven. Did he mean his wild woman went to Heaven this morning, too?

Travis didn't say a word for a long minute. "I'm sorry for your loss."

Joe gestured wildly. "You don't understand. You just don't know. She died in the night." He gritted his teeth. "I didn't know what to do. Me and the guys talked it over and decided to bury her. We dug a grave in the sand and put her in it. I left her there."

A tension filled silence blanketed the room, heavy, uncomfortable. Sara Beth was afraid to move, to swallow, or even breathe. Everything seemed louder than usual. She could even hear a bird singing in the chinaberry tree outside the window. The clock on the mantle ticked loudly making every minute longer.

Travis's voice, deep, and very stern rang out. "What do you mean you buried her on the beach?"

"We put her in the ground and covered her up," Joe said and shrugged. "We didn't know what else to do."

"Man!" Travis shook his head and straightened in his chair. "You should have informed the police." He stared across at Joe. "Are you certain she was dead? She may have been merely unconscious."

"No. She was dead," Joe insisted. The flare of the sun streaked through the window across his face, his expression wild, scary.

"How do you know that?" Travis' voice rang with skepticism, firm, and filled with authority.

Joe stopped pacing and stared at Travis, distracted as if viewing the woman again. "She was cold as ice to the touch, and she wasn't breathing. No pulse either. I tried to bring her to, but I couldn't wake her up." Joe hung his head. "The other guys made me stop. Said she was gone." He held out his hands palms up, defeated. "That was all."

"I say again, you should have gone to the authorities. Why didn't you?"

Joe glared at Travis. "Cause I might get blamed. I brought her to the party."

"For Pete sakes, Joe, if she died in her sleep, you weren't to blame for that." Travis raised his chin and studied Joe. "Did you do something to her to cause some injury?"

The grim tones of the men's voices made Sara Beth afraid. She wanted to get up and run away, but she couldn't. Her daddy would be pretty mad if he found out she'd been listening. She held her breath for a second, slowly exhaling.

"No, I tell you. She was just dead when I woke up." Joe retraced his steps and stared out the window at the front lawn, or maybe the chinaberry tree. "The other guys helped me bury her. None of 'em wanted to go to the cops, either."

After a long interval, Travis suggested, "Even now, you should go to the police."

Joe twisted around to face Travis, his hands in his pockets jingling coins with a nervous twitch. "It's too late for that. I'd go to jail. Maybe never get out."

Sara Beth studied Joe's face. His features were sort of crumpled and sad, but determined, stubborn even. Her daddy couldn't make him listen. Sara Beth wanted to shake her head, but remembered not to call notice to her hiding spot.

She sighed under her breath. Joe was willful, like her sometimes. She glanced at her daddy. She'd seen that look before. It was the same one he wore when trying to reason with her mama—after some of their little talks.

Travis took a deep breath through his teeth. "Her family will need to be notified. What are you going to tell them?"

With a jerk, Joe raised both hands up into the air. "Nothing. She don't have any family, least ways, not around here. No kids, no mate, no relatives as far as I know. If she did, she didn't say."

Travis stared at him. "Do you know anything about her?"

"Not much. I met her in a bar. She said she liked flowers. Since Marigolds were her favorite, I could call her Marigold." Joe shrugged. "That's all I know."

Travis edged to the front of his seat, his voice urgent, "What if I go with you? We can take my car and I'll help you tell the story. I know you have a hard time being understood occasionally."

Joe stopped jingling the coins, his gaze directed at the carpet. "That's decent of you, but no. I can't risk it."

"What if I call and report the death for you?"

Joe stared at Travis. "And what will you say. Someone told you a woman died on the beach. You think the police will be interested in some drifter from parts unknown?" He shook his head. "No siree, they won't."

"Well, calm yourself and sit down. You make me nervous with your pacing. I'll put the coffeepot on."

On his way to the kitchen, Travis must have caught sight of the ruffle on her pink dress. "Sara Beth. Come out here, young lady."

Slowly crawling out from behind the chair, she bumped the side-table making the ivory lamp shade tremble. She stood before her daddy with her hands gripped behind her back and her head down.

"Sara Beth, go to your room." He pointed his finger, his arm long and stiff.

She dared a peek at his face. His features were stern. Maybe his eyebrows were scrunched together because he was mad. She couldn't tell. Turning away, she slowly shuffled across the dining-room floor to the hall. It took her a long time to reach her bedroom door. She could still hear their voices, but she couldn't understand what Joe said from this far away.

"Shucks," she muttered, soft and low. She'd heard her mama say something like it, but she couldn't say that word. She was in enough trouble.

Opening the door to her room, she reluctantly entered. She knew she had to stay there. Daddy said so.

"Oh well," she mumbled to the room at large. Shrugging, she glanced around waiting to see if the strange, disturbing sensation hid in this room too. It didn't, at least, at the moment.

Studying the pink ruffles around the bottom of the coverlet on her bed, and at the windows, she smiled. Sara Beth loved pink, and her white princess bedstead. A special picture of a ballerina wearing a pink tutu hung on her wall, all gold-framed and pretty. She loved dancing, too. Her mama knew all of that about her.

She sighed and dragged her feet across the polished floor to the window. Placing her elbows on the sill and resting her chin on her hands, she watched, waiting until Clutch, er, Joe headed to his truck again. The same disturbing disquiet overwhelmed her. She had been wrong. It hadn't disappeared, yet. Dropping her head into her arms, she waited until Joe's truck fired up. When he drove out of sight, the sensation melted away.

Chapter 3

As the months passed, the strange, disturbing sensation floated through her life like smoke, faint, transparent, but no longer intense or overwhelming. Sara Beth didn't think about it anymore. Not even at night when she dreamed. Not even that night. Not until the next day. Not until her dream turned into a waking nightmare.

When Sara Beth drifted off to sleep, she viewed a young girl near her sister's age. Emily was her name and she had sandy colored hair with corkscrew curls passed her shoulders. Sara Beth liked the other girl's pretty green eyes and even the freckles that danced across her nose.

In her dream, Sara Beth watched Emily sitting in a pool of light cast by a glass lamp with Chinese symbols on the side. She and another girl were playing a game of Parcheesi. A little white dog with brown spots lay on the floor beside her. Nothing strange or frightening there, but the next day the vision, or dream or whatever was a different matter.

At her sister's heels, Sara Beth entered a house she'd never visited before. The strange, disturbing sensation returned, intense, overwhelming, snatching her breath away. The dream, her dream turned into a nightmare, real and scary.

Emily, the girl in Sara Beth's dream, sat on the floor in a pool of light playing Parcheesi with another girl. The light only brightened the center of the room. Dim shadows blanketed every inch outside the ring of light. With a now heightened awareness, Sara Beth sensed the shadows hovering over the girls.

"Gail, I wanna go home."

Her sister shook her head. "No. Don't be stupid."

Emily grinned at Sara Beth. "Come and play. Both of you."

Gail sank to the floor and crossed her legs ready to join the game, but Sara Beth shook her head. "Could we raise the window shades? It's too dark to see."

Emily jumped up and pulled on the rolled shades until it flew to the top of the window. "There. That ought to do."

Sunlight poured into the room and the shadows retreated, but Sara Beth noticed dark shapes lingered in the dim corners. She still wanted to go home. She could see the Chinese décor of the room, the wallpaper, the furniture and that same lamp. Something fluttered in her stomach, sort of sick. To her, the shadows seemed to move, to hoover, and to threaten. Sara Beth couldn't wait to leave, but Gail took forever to stop playing.

Following her sister out of the house, Sara Beth determined never to enter that house again, not even to play with the cute little dog sitting on the steps. She wanted to pat his head, but then, she remembered the dog had been in the dream too—now the nightmare.

Thin wisps of smoke seemed to creep under the door right behind her. Glancing over her shoulder, she could see something that resembled heat waves floating in the air, scary, horrifying. A shudder raced down her back.

Hurrying to catch up with her sister, she said, "That place is creepy."

Gail grumbled. "It was not. You're acting like a baby because she was my friend, not yours. I'll never take you with me again."

"Good." Sara Beth raised her chin. "I didn't want to go anyhow. You know our mama made you take me with you." She walked a little faster.

Gail trailed behind. "Did not."

Sara Beth looked back at her. "Did too, but I don't care. I'm gonna run home as fast as I can."

Her sister taunted, "Go ahead, scaredy-cat."

Sara Beth dashed down the street spraying gravel beneath her tennis shoes. Trying hard to outdistance the threatening shadows, she couldn't outrun the menacing misty forms. Those dim shapes shimmered like rising heat waves at her heels all the way to her house. Fear twisted through her. She didn't understand why her sister wasn't afraid, too.

That night, afraid of the dark, the shadows, and a menacing presence, she couldn't go to sleep. She fought to remain awake until she could no longer keep her eyes open. Sleep overtook her, and just as she had feared, the dark forms chased her.

The next night and the next happened in the same manner. Sara Beth sat in a chair trying to force her eyelids to stay open. The heat waves were chasing her again. She screamed when one grabbed her by the shoulder.

"Sara Beth. Wake up. You're crying in your sleep. What's wrong, baby?"

Sara Beth rubbed her eyes with the backs of her hands. "I don't want to sleep anymore. Not ever again."

Her mother, sweet smelling as always, wrapped her arms around Sara Beth. "Honey, you need to sleep. Everyone needs sleep. You can't go on without rest– and that means sleep. That's when your body repairs itself."

Sara Beth climbed up into her mama's lap. "But shadows chase me. They are white, sometimes thick and then thin. If I don't keep awake, they'll get me."

"How can a shadow be white?"

"I don't know, but these are. They are after me." Sara Beth gestured with her hands, palms up.

Her mama gave her a little squeeze. "Do you see yourself in these nightmares?"

Sara Beth nodded.

"Then run into your room and slam the door on whatever is chasing you. You can even turn to key if you want. This nightmare creature can't get in if you don't let it."

Sara Beth looked at her mama pulling her lips tight. Grownups didn't understand anything. Her mama sure didn't. "But the nightmare starts in my room. If I lock the door, I'll trap the shadows in with me."

"Make this shadow chase you out of the room. Then, when the creature, whatever it is, follows you, run back inside as quick as you can and shut the door."

The next morning Sara Beth stretched awake. She managed to lock the shadows out. She jumped up and ran to her mama. "Your suggestion worked. The shadows bang on the door now, but they can't get in." She grinned. "Only thumping real loud, but that's all."

"Well, that's a blessing. You can sleep now." Mama pushed up from the couch.

"What are you gonna do?"

"I'm doing the wash. Why don't you play with your paper-dolls? I'll give you a call and let you help me hang the laundry on the line when I'm finished."

That afternoon, while playing on the front porch, Sara Beth circled the white column with one arm and swung around it. She jumped to the first concert step and back again. Heat waves began to thicken. *Oh no!* The hairs on the back of her neck stood up. She knew something was going to happen.

Gail came running down the road, the gravel dust flying up behind her. Sara Beth hurried to the edge of the driveway and waited. A whiff of wild honeysuckle floated on a gentle breeze from the woods behind the house. Maybe Gail would climb the big white oak tree with her. That would be fun. Her mama wouldn't let her climb, even to the first limb, by herself. No matter how much she begged, her mama always said not by herself.

Gail arrived, out of breath and shaking all over. Dust covered her shoes and coated her book satchel as well. In her hurry, she must have dragged it on the ground.

Sara Beth frowned. Her sister looked hot and frazzled. "What's wrong?"

Gail didn't answer. Not even when Sara Beth followed her in the door. The musty smell of dust followed her sister inside the house too.

Gail flung her satchel on the couch and called, "Mama."

"I'm in the kitchen." Mama came to the door wiping her hands on a dish towel. She took one look at Gail and demanded, "What has happened?"

"It's a mad dog," Gail stammered. "It bit Emily's dog. Nobody was home to let her pet inside. I ran as fast as I could."

"When did this happen?"

"Right now. I was afraid the mad dog would get me. It had rabies all foaming at the mouth and staggering. After the mad dog bit Emily's pet, it fell down and had a fit. I ran as fast as I could. The mad dog followed me down the street, staggering sort of blind like."

Mama dialed the pound reporting the incident to the authorities. At that moment, our dog Skip began to howl.

"Oh," Mama groaned. "I should have thought to bring Skip into the house."

The sounds of a fierce fight, dogs snarling, terrified yelping, and growling pierced into the house. Sara Beth headed to the door.

"Don't you dare open that door, Sara Beth. It's dangerous. Besides, it's too late now."

"Why is it too late?" Sara Beth wanted to know, tears rolling down her cheeks.

"After a rabid dog bites a dog or another animal, like Skip, then the one bitten is infected with rabies and can give it to others, including people. I can't allow that to happen. Skip must be put down."

"But we love Skip," Sara Beth wailed, desolate at the thought of losing Skippy. That was her special name for him. Now this! Her chest clenched with pain.

"I know sweetheart, but we have no choice."

Sara Beth wondered if Emily would cry and feel bad when her dog had to be put down too. Those blasted heat waves. This was their fault. She wished those monsters would go away and never come back.

Chapter 4

Wispy trails of smoke or heat waves still brushed against Sara Beth from time to time, but on the whole, she managed to ignore the sensations. Months later in the middle of the night, the disturbing strangeness overwhelmed her again in full force. A loud thumping sounded outside the bedroom window. Sara Beth and her sister scooted into Mama and Daddy's room. Both girls crawled into bed between their parents.

Sara Beth shivered. "Mama, it's happening out loud. That's the nightmare I told you about. It's scary like I said."

The pounding grew louder much like a sledge hammer swung by an enraged giant determined on wrecking the house. Both her mama and daddy bolted upright in bed.

"What in the world is that?" Travis swung his legs over the side and stood up reaching for his flashlight. "You girls stay here. I'm going to see what's happening."

The thumping continued, stopped and started again louder than before. It seemed to come from inside the wall. After a while, Travis entered the bedroom and sank onto the edge of the bed.

"There isn't a single pipe or wire inside that particular wall." He shrugged. "I have no idea of what could be causing such a racket."

Mama suggested, hope in her voice, "Maybe the sound will stop soon."

Daddy said, "You girls may sleep with us until the pounding goes away. I can investigate better tomorrow when there's more light."

The next day, Daddy called the police to report the strange occurrence. When the police car arrived all black and white with red lights on top, Sara Beth rushed outside behind her daddy. She didn't want to miss anything, especially what the policeman would do about the pounding.

The officer listened to the thumping and wrote out a report, but Sara Beth noticed he had a scared look on his face. He lost no time in leaving, even to the point of spinning out and making the gravel in the drive scatter.

The thumping continued night and day for several days fraying everyone's nerves. Finally, the noise stopped. The entire family followed Travis out the door to find out what had happened to make the sound quit. A small section of the siding beside the window was shattered as if a tiny bomb had exploded inside the wall. The strange, disturbing sensation no longer overwhelmed Sara Beth. The sensations seemed to have disappeared with the noise—she hoped forever.

In time, now busy raising her own family, Sara Beth pushed such happenings to the back of her consciousness. A small tingle of awareness always lingered, sensitive, alert callings of caution. Vapors, thin and slightly hazy, brushed against her from time to time, but nothing like before.

Years later, Hurricane Ike swept through Galveston leaving a wake of destruction behind. The storm had a powerful wind force and a torrent of rain. Big, wide and intense, Ike devoured entire communities on the island. Sara Beth hoped the hurricane would dissipate soon. With enough sea water to kill all of the trees lining the boulevard leading down to the ocean, the hurricane raged inland straight up I-45 taking days to lessen into a tropical storm.

Cleaning up the devastation took time and effort. For several days afterwards, pictures of the destruction appeared on the news, gut-wrenching to Sara Beth. Watching television where people cried at the loss of loved ones, homes, and jobs, she was grateful she and her family had only lost a few giant oak trees. Many had escaped with only the clothes on their backs. It was a sad time. The cleanup started as soon as the last raindrop fell.

Days later, the strange, disturbing sensation overwhelmed Sara Beth once more. She sat in her own home, her attention glued to the TV. A pretty, blonde reporter from Channel 2 News reported the skeleton of a woman had been uncovered at a construction site on the beach. The authorities considered the bones had been in the ground for fifty years or more.

Sara Beth knew in her knower the skeleton belonged to Marigold. A shame that her relatives, if any existed, would never know what happened to her. Her wasted life, her true identity, and why she died in the night would all remain a mystery, but at least, someone knew of her passing.

Since that time, Sara Beth thought of Marigold now and again. There was nothing she could do to identify the remains. Daddy had passed on long ago, a few years after her mama. She had no idea of the identity of the hair-lipped man named Joe, and doubted he still lived.

Sara Beth took a deep breath and sighed. This was one of the true incidents never to be solved—a real life mystery. She never considered she might have Extrasensory perception better known as ESP. To her, the sensations were more akin to knowing, simply knowing. She only prayed the disturbing, breath-taking sensations wouldn't overtake her again. Not now, not in her mature years, not ever again.

The End

About the Author-Wareeze Woodson

I write historical romance fiction novels set in the 1800s forward with a twist of suspense. All of my characters and stories that are portrayed in my books are fictitious. I am a native of Texas, but I have traveled throughout America and beyond. As a dreamer, I love to visit new places where I can imagine a heroine meeting a hero in a special way. I'm an avid reader of all sorts and I love to write. I married my high school sweetheart and after having raised three sons plus one daughter, our love for each other remains unshaken. Now we enjoy our eight grandchildren. We can send them home, but we're always happy for their return. Outside of my family activities, I sing with the Silver Belles at my church and hate to miss even one practice. The local chapter of RWA is also at the top of my list of pleasures. It keeps me grounded with craft and connected with other writers. Most of all, I enjoy going fishing with my husband. Give me a pole and leave me alone to bask in the sun, listening to water gurgle along the riverbanks while allowing my mind to float away to some distance place. Ah! Perfect.

(Editor's Note: I first met Wareeze though her historical romance, "Conduct Unbecoming a Gentleman." I loved it and we stayed in touch.

Shortly after this bio was written, tragedy stuck Wareeze's adored husband. Diagnosed and stricken with a terrible illness, he died quickly, within a week's time.

After some months of grief had passed we asked Wareeze to write for us again. She wasn't sure how it would go. But, the shivery story you have just read is the wonderful result! She says it is based on true historical events. Can you imagine?

Thank God, Wareeze is recovering. But, you can encourage her by reading her published novels.

In time, we hope more and even better novels will come along. In the meantime, we recommend any great read from the following list.)

Books by Wareeze Woodson
US Go Here: http://amzn.to/2xikwlu
UK Go Here: http://amzn.to/2xinqGU

Conduct Unbecoming of a Gentleman

Recently widowed, Lady Laurel Laningham flees Landings to escape her untenable position. Alone now and at the mercy of her sister-in-law, she decides to nestle under her aunt's wings for a spell. To add to her burdens, Laurel's young son's new guardian, Lord Adron Gladrey, has announced his intentions to take complete charge of his ward.

An Enduring Love

Born and raised in Latvia, Rebecca Balodis marries Rhys Sudduth, an English diplomat. Shortly thereafter, he is summoned home to attend his father's deathbed. Rebecca cannot accompany him at the time and becomes trapped in the turmoil plaguing her country. He is informed she died in the upheaval.

Books by Wareeze Woodson
US Go Here: http://amzn.to/2xikwlu
UK Go Here: http://amzn.to/2xinqGU

A Lady's Vanishing Choices

After running away, Bethany Littleton, alone in a forest, witnesses a man burying a roll large enough to hold a corpse. She thinks she has escaped undetected, but danger follows her.

After She Became a Lady

Laurel Collingsworth, seventeen and deeply in love, expects to marry her hero and live in wedded bliss forever after. Instead, with the ink barely dry on the marriage lines, Lord Robert Laningham is called away to Spain and the war.

We'll See

Myron McDonald

One of the great events of the early farm society—which was prone to seize every excuse for get-togethers of any kind but which was, in its Christian work-ethic ethos, particularly pleased when business could, so to speak, be combined with pleasure—was the autumn ritual of threshing.

Today, with the family unit giving way to the mathematics of agriculture as a mass production business, the giant self-propelled combine has made harvesting about as romantic as truck driving.

But, in the heyday of my grandmother, threshing was it.

There were generally two parts to this great excitement. Oats ripened early and their awned heads bowed weeks before the wheat was ready. But oats were not a cash crop; so, most family farmers planted just enough to enrich the diet of millet or clover hay fed the work horses as a staple. "Hay, while idle; oats while working" was the octane rule for this internal combustion engine.

Wheat was the big small-grain crop. The emotion attendant on the harvest of a successful wheat planting was the equal of the Vendemia which begins the grape harvest in Jerez, the heart of the Spanish sherry country; though perhaps not so flamboyant—there was no bishop in Calhoun County, Michigan.

In the depth of the Great Depression a man's hold on his farm often depended on the success of his wheat crop. But, at any time, the pre-harvest conversation was heady and mysterious to a ten year old.

"This year, we'll hold it," my grandmother would say.

"Well, Hat, I don't know," my step-grandfather would reply.

One of the buildings on my grandmother's farm was a granary. It featured huge wooden bins with individually removable front boards and a delicious, somehow reassuring smell, when it was full of the new harvest.

In the spring, with the oats a thin scatter at the bottom of two bins and only stray golden kernels in the wheat storage, the air was apt to turn musty-dusty.

When the first car on the farm replaced Old Jack, the buggy horse of fifteen years tenure, we drove the Model T into the space where the wagons backed in the fall to deliver their newly-threshed load to the bins. As I grew older I learned to judge the relative economic health of the farm in late winter and early spring by the level of the grain. If the bins were half full or more, things were pretty good. Most springs they were Mother Hubbard's cupboard. Throughout my recollection of eight or nine summers on the farm, a running theme of contention between my grandparents was whether to sell the wheat crop at once or wait, in the hope of a better price.

Since many farmers were forced by their constant need for cash to send the threshing wagons directly to the nearest grain-buying elevator, dribbling en-route a thin trickle of gold which turned immediately into a line of happy birds, the price of wheat was usually depressed during the first weeks of the harvest and those who could "hold it" for demand to catch up with supply were reckoned fortunate.

Then came October, 1929, and in its wake a series of years when prices went down and down and down until a bushel--58 pounds--of first-grade red, hard bread-flour wheat sold for less than the cost of twenty filter cigarettes today. And, as often as not, those who "held it" got a lower price.

"Remember what happened to August Seifert," my step-grandfather would say, hoping to end the argument he knew he did not have the bottom to win if it went on.

Sifert was a thrifty German-American whose farm was a model of industry and tidiness. He was always one who "held it." In the year referred to by Frank, wheat had nose-dived following the Bank Holiday and Siefert, the ant, had taken twenty cents a bushel less than the improvident grasshoppers who had had to rush their crop to the mill directly from the threshing machine.

"That goddammed Roosevelt," my grandmother would reply.

"Let's talk about it later, Hat."

"We'll see, Frank, we'll see."

As a compromise, they would walk out and look at the crop if it were a near field, or ride if it happened this year to be the back forty.

This was a solemn occasion and I tagged along knowing to listen.

"Looks good, Frank," my grandmother would say at the edge of the gold. "Think it'll go thirty bushels?"

My step-grandfather would remove his sweat stained straw hat, run his free hand over the dead white strip of his upper forehead and brush his hair back from a frown of concentration--tall, handsome man beside a short, wiry woman in calico to her ankles, sunbonnet flapping to accent her question.

"Don't know, Hat. It does look good. But there's quite a thin spot in the hollow next to the woods where it drowned out."

"Frank, you've got to get some drain tile in there!"

Maybe twenty-eight or twenty-nine bushels," he replied, hurrying now past the chore of digging a hundred yards of ditch for the tile, hoping my grandmother would disremember.

"We'll see."

About the Author-Myron McDonald

Myron C. McDonald, was born and raised in Calhoun County in Southern Michigan, USA. Later he attended college and met his future wife, June, at Michigan State University. While attending college on a shoestring, he washed dishes for his upkeep. The first and only college graduate in his family, Myron went on to success as an advertising executive, rising to the post of Vice President of the huge New York firm, McCann Erickson. After retirement, Myron and June spent their remaining years in comfort, in Tucson, Arizona where he died in the year 2000. Myron's memoirs of his grandmother Harriette were written about 1970 and never published. The original work was entitled, "That Tough Little Lady, My Grandmother." The current work, "He Called Her Hat," has been edited, adapted and designed by Dorothy May Mercer, author of several published works.

The #1 Matriarch - Margaret Basler Reiss Ebert

Steve Reiss

Dear Mercer Publications;
I would like to offer the attached story that I emailed to our four young grandchildren. It's from my book, It Takes A Matriarch, published in 2009 by Author House.
Thanks,
Steve

The #1 Matriarch - Margaret Basler Reiss Ebert

Steve Reiss

August 18, 2014
Dear Will, Kayla, Ava, and Blake,

Your great great great great grandmother Margaret Basler was born on 10/22/1818 in the picturesque Swiss village of Niederzeihen (lower Zeihen).
She was the second of ten children and the oldest daughter. Her father Johann Basler was the village mayor, burgermeister, or gemeindeammann.

The Swiss village of Niederzeihen (lower Zeihen

This photo was their house near the village center.

Johann, his wife Katharina and eight of their surviving children as family number 292308, arrived in New Orleans on 11/28/1839 from Le Havre, France on a ship called Salem. Their oldest son Nicholaus had previously arrived at the same port in 1836 and now lived in Louisville, Kentucky.

The Basler family quickly moved north to settle in the German community of Paderborn, Illinois about two miles from a 40-acre farm owned by a widower J. (Johann) Adam Reiss.

Adam had built his log cabin on his Illinois farm, as well as an adjacent log granary. Both measured about 15 feet by 18 feet and had stone foundations. During the fall of 1836 he had moved in along with his pregnant wife Mary. Their son John was born in December 1838 but sadly Mary died during that childbirth.

Adam hosted Catholic Church services on his farm in his log cabin, his log granary, or outdoors as the seasons allowed. He did that for about two years and most likely started that practice with Mary.

Those church services may have been where the Basler and Reiss families first met in late 1839. So here was Margaret age twenty--the oldest Basler child in the area. And there was Adam Reiss age 34, new landowner, handyman farmer, and widower with an infant son.

Somehow, it made sense. Margaret and Adam were married that same year.

In a few months she had gone from an upscale house with wooden floors in Switzerland, to a very small log cabin with a dirt floor in Illinois, becoming a wife, homemaker and step-mom with an infant son.

Awesome lady!!!

Margaret soon became pregnant. Unfortunately, her mother, Katharina, had died in March, only six months after the wedding. Still no more than a bride, now pregnant, as a stepmother to a three year old, and married to Adam, a man fourteen years older than herself. Margaret became the family matriarch at the age of twenty-two.

Happily, their son Frank Joseph Reiss was safely born on September 27th.

It helped some, when in December, her father, Johann Basler, bought a forty-acre farm northeast of Paderborn. Although Margaret's mother was gone, this meant her siblings were closer, now.

It wasn't long before Margaret's next younger sister Sophia married nearby farmer Frantz Stauder, the following March. He was also a recent widower and was raising two small children under the age of five.

With two toddlers clinging to her skirts, Margaret gave birth to two more sons, Charles Joseph, in 1843, and Martin Charles, two years later. She now had three sons and one step-son, under the age of five.

Meanwhile, her father Johann Basler sold his farm and left the area, with his unmarried children, moving to Louisville, Kentucky.

Adam and Margaret, seemingly unable to quit, kept having children every two years. Now with four sons, their first daughter Catharine Reiss was born in 1847, but their second, Barbara Reiss was stillborn sometime in 1849.

Alas, no more children came, because Margaret's husband Adam Reiss died of cholera on May 23, 1849.

Margaret was now a widow at age thirty, with five children ages two to ten, living in a small log cabin with dirt floor, on a 120 acre farm. Can you imagine!!!

~~*~*~*~*

The next decade of the 1850s was kinder to Margaret but still had major highs and lows.

Margaret married Conrad Ebert in April, 1850. He was older than her by seven years, having been born in Germany in 1811. He had arrived in New Orleans in 1847 at the age of 36.

Their first daughter, her third, was born a year later. However Anna Maria Ebert did not reach adulthood because she is not mentioned in the 1860 census.

Margaret's fourth daughter, Louisa Ebert, was born in 1853 and her fifth, Margaret Ebert came along in 1856. Her last child, born in 1859 did not survive.

Her father Johann Basler had died in late 1854 in Louisville, Kentucky.

Meanwhile, Margaret and Conrad Ebert bought another forty acres to square off their farm at 160 acres. A final purchase of twenty more acres was added in 1868 on the northeast corner of their farm.

Margaret's two adventuresome younger brothers moved to California in 1852.

The first, George Anselm Basler, took a steamship from New York to Panama, crossed the isthmus, and took a second steamship to San Francisco. He later participated in gold rushes in Nevada and British Columbia.

The second, Martin Basler, his wife Anna Maria, and two month old son John took a covered wagon for 105 days along the California Trail from St. Joseph, Missouri to Sacramento.

The next four decades of the 1860s through the 1890s included additional joys and sorrows.

After her brother Nicholaus Basler died in 1860 in Louisville, Margaret was now the oldest of seven surviving Basler siblings.

Son John Reiss married Maria Josephine Gass in 1861 and had ten children but lost four of them one week in May 1888 to disease.

Fighting in the Civil War with four different Illinois regiments were Margaret's brother George Basler, sons John and Frank Reiss and son-in-law Charles Max Wittig. All returned but two were wounded.

After her younger sister Sophia Basler Stauder died in1865, Margaret became the only Basler living in Illinois. Her parents were deceased. Two brothers were in California, two sisters were in St. Louis, one brother was in a Civil War veterans' home in Dayton, Ohio and one brother was in Sullivan, Indiana.

Son Frank Reiss married Anna Antonia Syvilla Feder in 1866 and had eleven children but only seven reached adulthood.

Daughter Kate Reiss married Charles Max Wittig in the double ceremony with her brother Frank and Anna. They had five daughters with four reaching adulthood.

1866 was a big year for weddings. Margaret's son Charles Reiss married Eva Dintelmann and had seven children with all seven reaching adulthood.

A daughter Louisa Ebert's life ended in tragedy. After marrying George W. Neff in November 1873 and bearing him one son, she died less than two years later when her clothes caught fire while making apple butter.

Daughter Margaret Ebert married George's younger brother, Charles, in 1877 and had five children who all reached adulthood.

At last, Margaret became a widow for the second time when her husband, Conrad Ebert, died in 1880 at the age of sixty-nine.

Three brothers pre-deceased Margaret. Two younger brothers died in California. Martin Basler died in 1881 in Sacramento, California, while George Anselm Basler died in 1888 in San Francisco. Her older brother Johann Jakob "George" Basler died in 1897 in Dayton, Ohio.

The last son to marry, Martin Reiss married Margaret Williams in 1883 and had three children but only one reached adulthood. Their marriage was rather short-lived. Margaret died in 1891 and Martin in 1898.

The 1900 census shows Margaret with five of her ten children still living. Stepson John was the first born, then five children with Adam Reiss, and four more with Conrad Ebert.

~~*~*~*~

Dear Will, Kayla, Ava, and Blake:

Our matriarch Margaret saved 780 letters written between 1852 and 1888. The many writers were her siblings and spouses, her Reiss children, several grandchildren, and two friends. Only 22 of these letters were written by Margaret. Most were written in "old" German and were translated between 2004 and 2008. About twenty percent of the letters are in phonetic English and are just plain fun to read. All these letters were published by Author House in 2009 in a book titled, *It Takes A Matriarch*. There are an amazing 412,000 words, a dozen photos, and 600 pages.

These letters show a consistent and very conscientious pattern of caring, leading, counseling, listening, sharing, and compassion. Margaret Basler Reiss Ebert was an outstanding matriarch, patriarch, and big sister. She was my great-great grandmother and simply a great person. I hope to meet her in heaven some day! Here's her book and her obituary.

Love, Granddad

It Takes A
Matriarch

763 Family Letters from 1852 to 1888
Including Civil War, Farming in Illinois,
Life in St. Louis, Life in Sacramento,
Life in the Theater, Wagon Making in Davenport,
and the Lost Family Fortune

By Stephen W. Reiss

 Huebinger Bros   DAVENPORT, IA.

Here is Margaret's obituary as translated from a local German newspaper:

In the Prairie du Long Township died on Sunday morning Mrs. Margaretha Ebert at an age of 84 years and nine months. Mrs. Ebert's maiden name was Margaretha Basler. She was the widow of Mr. Conrad

Ebert. At the time of her death, Mrs. Ebert was living on the farm of her daughter, Mrs. Conrad Neff, two miles north of Hecker.

Mrs. Ebert was born in Switzerland and came to the United States in the year 1839. Her first husband Mr. Adam Reiss died in 1849. Her second husband Mr. Conrad Ebert died in 1880.

Mrs. Ebert is survived by her children: John Reiss in Belleville, Frank Reiss in Floraville, Charles on the Ridge Prairie, Martin in Missouri, Mrs. Max Wittig in Davenport, Ia. and Mrs. Conrad Neff as well as 31 grandchildren and three great-grandchildren. Also her sisters Mrs. Charles Krone and Mrs. Samuel Perrow (*who died a week apart in July 1907*).

The funeral service was Wednesday morning at 8:00 o'clock in the Catholic Church in Hecker and the burial took place right after the service at St. Augustine Cemetery.

About the Author-Steve Reiss

Steve and Diane at Habitat for Humanity

On Palm Sunday, April 1, 2012, I was in church listening to the choir when I realized I was more than sixty-five years older than our, then, two grandchildren. Now I'm more than seventy years older than the last two grandchildren. Sadly, we are never going to have heavy adult conversations on family history, favorite stories, old photos, travel, fun times, hobbies, etc. So I resolved on that Palm Sunday to send two email stories every Monday to our grandchildren as attachments on emails to their parents. That resolution is still intact after five years and ten days. There have been 615 stories so far. I call them "Granddad's Mondays." Writing them is a fantastic blessing in my retirement years.

Baby Steve looking at his Dad's photo.

Memoirs/Personal Essay

Mr. Hill's Ark

Barbara Chamberlain

"The shack" was the most fascinating place in my five-year-old world. Our neighbor, who lived four houses from us, perfected recycling years ahead of its current popularity. The "work-in-progress" house was made of varicolored siding. Thompson seedless grape vines, buzzing with bees when the grapes ripened, covered the sky blue backyard picket fence. Mr. Hill found everything, including the sky blue paint, beachcombing the railroad tracks about eighty yards in back of our homes in Fresno.

My mother called Mr. Hill's house "that shack."

Two or three boxcar men usually would be hoteling in Mr. Noah Hill's backyard.

The men came from the trains that clattered by so often that I sometimes did not hear them. There must have been a mark or word of mouth leading them from the boxcars to Mr. Hill's. I traced their well-worn path through the ragweed, purple lupine, and golden poppies from the tracks to the ark. Because he was Noah, it all reminded me of a picture of the animals walking into Noah's ark, except the men walked one by one.

In1941 these men were looking for work, any work. Field work was abundant in California's Central Valley in the summer.

84

The men took any discarded item they found around the tracks to Mr. Hill's treasure stores. What did not fall off the railroad cars that roared by our homes twenty times a day was gleaned from the side of the field next to a road at the end of our block. People too lazy to drive to the dump threw paint cans, boards, old newspapers, even towels and clothes, etc. Mr. Hill and friends did the neighborhood a favor by dragging the clutter to the blue picket fence that separated his property from the field, which must have been owned by the railroad.

His back yard was lawn-challenged dirt polka-dotted with scrubby weeds.

The picket fence that matched my height guarded two chrome kitchen tables and a melting pot of chairs. Three railroad lanterns hung from the roof. Next to the little room that housed the toilet was an outside sink and counter. Mr. Hill probably regretted ever letting me into that room. What seemed like a hundred feet up to my five-year-old self was a huge white tank on the wall. To flush the toilet I could barely reach the CHAIN, which I adored pulling.

Mr. Hill's cooking methods were more captivating than THE TOILET.

My approach to his backyard was through the field. I was never in his house so Mr. Hill may not have had a kitchen. The outside stove for him and the men was a coffee can full of black oil, which Mr. Hill lit with his cigarette. The meal was usually a loaf of soft, soft white bread. The men tore off pieces and rolled them into doughy balls.

A ball was speared on the end of a stick and roasted black in the flaming oil.

Like a baby bird, I ate any black ball offered to me. It tasted like burnt bread spiced with oil. Today I would probably gag if anyone offered me an oil smoked ball of bread. That was then. This is now.

Grapes that grew on everyone's fences would wash away the taste of the oil.

"There but for the grace of God," Mom would say. My father had a job as a railway mail clerk. Not until I was attending college did I learn that he quit Stanford engineering a semester before graduation because he got that steady postal job during the Great Depression.

That's how much people needed jobs.

Never told my mother about eating at Mr. Hill's but I must have gone home often with a black tongue. Today's children would not be allowed to roam like that and hang out with men fresh from riding the rails. Hobos. My mom was busy with my baby sister and the constant stream of diapers that she put through the wringer washer.

Her parenting advice: "Go out and play." On those hot Central Valley days, the men accepted me like a long lost friend.

"You remind them of their families," Mr. Hill explained. "They're lonesome away from home. They know I always have an open door."

Like the ark story, Noah gave them a safe place with shelter from the storm.

"I'd be just like them except my aunt left me this lot. I'm good at building."

He told me this as I watched him lick the edge of a small square of paper, shake in some tobacco from a white pouch he carried in his shirt pocket, roll a cigarette, lick the paper's edge to make it stick. He lit it in the dying oil can flame.

The round end glowed.

I could feel my eyes widen as I stared at the red ash.

He puffed. To my delight he blew a smoke ring into the air. The ring grew larger and larger in the sky until it vanished.

The annual siege of the thick winter fog forced me inside. The invading mist hugged the ground so completely that a person could come within three feet me and materialize out of the gray like a ghost. Few men stopped at Mr. Hill's house. They were somewhere, like birds in a storm.

Only a man named Zeb stayed.

"Needs to rest. He's had a bad cough. The others have gone down south to the Imperial Valley to pick," Mr. Hill explained.

Housebound, I colored in my coloring books or listened to the radio. Even after my 8 p.m. curfew I could hear the radio plainly--Jack Benny, Fred Allen. I loved them all because they sounded like they were having so much fun.

One weekend in December, 1941, my nose started to run. Mother put me in bed.

She rubbed so much Vick's on my chest and throat that I drowned in the smell.

"Momma! That's awful!"

"We don't want you to get a cough, too." She pulled the covers to my nose.

"You probably won't be able to go to kindergarten."

I groaned. No finger painting, no show and tell, no pretending I was an elephant. I would miss child heaven.

Momma brought me a glass of hand-squeezed orange juice. In those days if you wanted orange juice you squeezed it. The juice was thick and pulpy. I barely made it to the bathroom to throw up. Momma washed my face and helped me back to bed.

Sure enough, by the next day I had created a Kleenex mountain. My head ached. Mom kept feeling my forehead. "Try to sleep."

"Could you turn on the radio?"

"This is Monday. I don't know what's on. Maybe soap operas."

"I can't sleep," I answered pitifully.

She disappeared into the living room to turn on the Philco.

After a few seconds we heard an announcer's voice, then President Roosevelt speaking. He talked on the radio every week. I never understood much of his speeches. But he had a nice voice.

"It's the president," I heard my mother say. "Why is he on now?"

"Last night Japanese forces attacked Guam. Last night Japanese forces attached the Philippine Islands and Midway Island..."

My mother's cry from the living room made me struggle to sit up.

"Momma, what is it?"

She did not answer.

"...as commander in Chief of the Army and Navy I have directed that all measures be taken for our defense. The American people in their righteous might will win through absolute victory. With confidence in our armed forces—with the unbounded determination of our people—we will gain the inevitable triumph; so help us God!"

He continued to talk. Momma came into the room with tears on her face.

"It is such awful news!"

I was trying to understand why the president was making my mother cry when the wall phone in the hall rang.

The phone rang three more times. I kept expecting more rings because my mother had four sisters and a brother who all lived in Fresno.

As I slowly recovered, the world had changed even to a five year old. Two of my aunts were working at Hammer Airfield rigging parachutes. Uncle Bill was going to be a pilot. Uncle Harry was in the cavalry. We had a picture of him on his dark horse.

Even Zebediah left Mr. Hill's ark.

"He enlisted in the army," Mr. Hill told me.

"Will all your friends go in the Army? My uncles are in the Army."

I wondered if the first Noah stayed in the ark when everyone else left.

"Most are. I'm too old. I hear your pop's going down to the recruitment office."

He blew a smoke ring into the cold air.

Walking home through the brown, dried winter weeds I wondered if papa would be a soldier. When I looked up I saw that Mr. Hill's smoke ring was growing larger and larger until it was swallowed in the gray winter day. I clung to the fact that Noah Hill's ark would always be ready to give shelter from the storm in the outside world.

My Buddy
Sarah Gipson Award
Barbara Chamberlain

My son and I walked slowly through the cages at the animal shelter. My husband thought we needed a watchdog after our last dog had passed away. Eddie stopped abruptly at a cage. When I walked up a beautiful Irish Setter with huge brown eyes was staring at me through the black bars. The sign said, *four months old. Found by the side of the freeway.*

"Oh, Mom! Let's take this one. He'll be my buddy!"

I should have known something was not right when *My Buddy* threw up all over the back seat of the car going home. He also chewed up everything chewable in the backyard.

For his whole twelve years Buddy trembled and hid behind a tree when strangers came to our door. My husband was so embarrassed when he stood in lines at the pet store for Buddy's shots. The dog trembled the whole time as though he had been beaten every day. Any dog would envy the dream treatment he received from the age of four months.

Buddy grew into a gorgeous dog. He pranced when he ran. When he shook his head my husband swore he heard a sound like an empty rattle.

Eddie went off to college.

Buddy got old. One day he came in panting and flopped on the kitchen floor.

When he did not move for a few hours I told my husband that he might have had a stroke. I gave him water and broth with a turkey baster. Moving was so

90

difficult for him, but he was such a good guy that he always dragged himself outside for his bathroom routines. He came back, panting and flopped on the floor again.

"I don't think Buddy is going to make it," my husband said. "We need to get him to the vet's. I'm going to dig a grave."

Our backyard is a third of an acre. In the far back is a pet cemetery with a dozen cats and dogs that have lived with us over the years. My husband went out to dig the grave.

A grave for a dog like Buddy needed to be almost people sized. It was quite a project to make it three feet deep.

That night Buddy, who was on his bed by ours, started to whimper that he wanted out.

"He's such a good guy," my husband said. "As hard as it is he doesn't want to make a mistake in the house. He doesn't go far. I'll let him out."

But he did not return. I checked the clock, "Buddy's been gone for half an hour."

We started to hear the whimpering from the far back of our yard. The flashlight lit our way to the sound. Buddy had taken a Scrooge-like tumble into his grave and could not escape.

After we hauled him out the setter started to run like crazy around the backyard. The next day the old Buddy was back, racing across the fields, barking at birds flying by, hiding behind trees when people came to the house. Scared to life, he lived for another year.

Excerpt from Barbara Chamberlain's novel:

A Slice of Carmel
A Jaden Steele Mystery

... one way or another. Several of her customers like Ruth, were living on the edge of Carmel, on the edge of a town of well-off citizens. They just got by one way or the other. Some were like Ruth, from families who had bought homes fifty years earlier and found themselves in million dollar homes with small incomes.

Rumors were that Ruth's husband had run off with someone about fifteen years earlier. No children. She lived, literally, on the edge of Carmel in a house that was built into a hill next to Pacific Grove. It must have two or even three levels of stairs. Jaden picked up an orchid there one day when Ruth was not feeling well. Every window of the living room was full of blooming orchids of a rainbow of colors.

Jaden remembered how she took a deep breath of admiration when she saw them. When the flower of the orchid in the shop window of a Slice of Carmel fell off, there was no way it would ever bloom again for Jaden. Ruth would bring it back here and it would magically send out a new spike and bloom again for her.

White, pink, orchid lavender, yellow, vari-colored yellow with red stripes like the one she had brought in today.

Jaden drew the knife down the file twice (to make it look good) and tested it on a strip of paper. The blade slid down easily. It would cut through meat like butter. She shivered briefly. Jaden was raised with knives. Her grandfather had shown her how to sharpen and help him make knives. Against her grandmother's protests, her grandfather taught her how to throw knives. She always carried her monarch torsion blade knife, usually in her pocket. It was not really all for protection. Her husband, Brett, had the knife specially made for her. Brett had been gone five years. The knife was all she had left of him besides their wedding picture. Sometimes if she was not looking at the picture his face eluded her. She felt disloyal to a man she loved.

At least she knew what happened to her husband. Poor Ruth would probably never know.

"They are nice and sharp now." Jaden wrapped the two knives back in the newspaper and put them back in Ruth's light blue storage bag.

The bell attached to the door of the shop rang. A thin woman dressed in gray slacks and a matching gray shirt came into the shop. She smiled nervously. Jaden saw that the left side of her face in front of her ear was bruised. "Laura, what happened?"

"Oh," Laura looked at the floor. "It was so clumsy of me. I left the kitchen cupboard door open and walked right into it. It looks worse than it is, really."

Jaden and Ruth looked at each other.

It wasn't long ago that Laura came in with a broken arm. That time she said she fell off her back step. Accidents do happen.

Laura and her husband, Jeff, ran a souvenir shop near Seventh and Dolores. Jaden thought that Laura really ran the shop because Jeff spent a lot of time in the Carmel Pub halfway between here and their shop, The Village Gift Store.

Jaden always felt uneasy around him. She knew she should not pay attention to her sixth sense.

Sometimes, though, it overwhelmed everything else. That was not all good. She learned the hard way when ghosts lured her into dangerous smuggling caves under the Bartlett house in Big Sur.

It was a deadly trap. All of her memories told her that the good spirits in the house, the ones who wanted her to solve a mystery, helped her escape.

There were evil spirits who caused the death of two innocent people. Jaden learned that evil is always lurking, delighting in causing problems and death if it can. That feeds its ego and delights in misery.

Jaden also learned something that she had tried to submerge. The truth seemed disloyal to her first husband, a man who had been her best friend.

There was a new love in her life. To admit that made her happier than she had been in years. After she moved from Nebraska, Jaden's lover turned out to be a lying womanizer. Jaden could have easily killed him herself, but someone beat her to it. *Never admitted that to anyone but herself.*

In Carmel she had so many good friends-Bobbi Jones, Hal Lamont, who owned their small shopping corner, Ruth Stennis and her son, retired General Stennis, MacKenzie, her lawyer who owned a vacation condo here, Sydney and Kyle, who owned the Mad Hatter's Café.

Looking at Laura she sensed that the woman needed a friend.

"Laura, would you like some coffee or tea? I have some of that raspberry tea from the Mad Hatter's."

"No, thank you," Laura's eyes darted back and forth. "I just came in to pick up the knives I left for sharpening. The shop is closed right now and I want to open it up before the noon crowd comes."

"How is business?" Ruth asked.

~~*~*

To order this exciting novel please click here: http://amzn.to/2vjpo8i

About the Author-Barbara Chamberlain

Barbara Chamberlain
123 Merideth Ct.
Aptos, CA 95003
831-688-3356
barbarac@got.net
Carousel21@hotmail.com
www.jadensteelemysteries.com

Barbara Chamberlain has published The Jaden Steele Mystery Series, set in the Monterey Bay area. The *Sword of Smuggler's Point* is the third mystery in the series. The first is *A Slice of Carmel* and the second Jaden Steele Mystery, *Slash and Turn*, introduced a visiting Russian ballet company whose members are the target of a murderer. The story leads readers through a maze to its final exciting conclusion

Barbara's juvenile fantasy, *The Flight of Alpha I,* won first place for fantasy in the 2014 National League of American Pen women literary contest.

Barbara's short story, Mall Santa, is included in *A Miracle Under the Christmas Tree*, released by Harlequin in October, 2012. She won first place in the juvenile/young adult category of the Writers' Digest Competition for her original fable set in Okinawa, *A Bowl of Rice.*

Barbara's first novels, *Ride the West Wind* and *The Prisoner's Sword*, were reprinted in 2011. They were named Recommended Reading by the National Council of Teachers of English. In 2009 Barbara's original fable set in Okinawa won First Place in the Writer's Digest Writing Competition. Her short story won first place in the Northern California Pen Women 2011 literary contest.

Barbara has taught storytelling and creative writing classes through adult schools and community college. At a large family genealogy conference in 2009 she facilitated a session, Telling Your Own Stories; Magic Through Memories. This was similar to a presentation done in 2007 at the NSN Sig Pre-Conference session as well as the Asilomar Reading conference in Pacific Grove. Performances have been at private parties, local organizations, the Monterey City Library's Tellabration, and the Palo Alto Children's Library Storytelling Festival. Rockin' Folktales is Barbara's CD of Middle Eastern stories.

As an elementary school librarian at Bradley Elementary School she set up three different libraries. Barbara also worked in youth services and reference at Monterey City Library and Harrison Memorial Library in Carmel. While working in Carmel she developed the concept for The Jaden Steele Mysteries set in the fascinating Monterey Bay area.

The University of California at Santa Cruz awarded Barbara a bachelor's degree in 1987. She received her Master's degree in Library and Information Science from San Jose University in 1992.

She is the past president of the Northern California Pen Women and is a member of the Santa Clara County Branch. She is currently First Vice District Governor of District 4C6 and a member of the local Cabrillo Host Lions Club. She and her husband, Dave, live in Aptos, California.

Please continue reading for an excerpt from Book 1 of Barbara's wildly popular Jaden Steele Series, *A Slice of Carmel*.

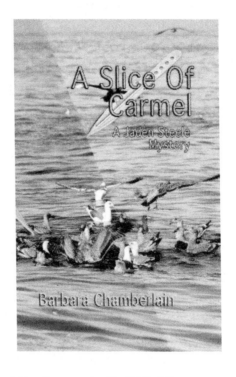

Go Here: http://amzn.to/2vCUbA0

Thanks Giving

Ron Shaw

Copyright © 2016 Ron Shaw

Thanks Giving is dedicated to three, lovely sisters, Brenda, Cathy, and Vicki.

Acknowledgements

Cover concept and design were created by the author. The background used for the cover is an artistic rendering offered as "CCO Public Domain", "Free for commercial use", "No attribution required" and courtesy of pixabay at http://www.pixabay.com.

Contents:

Thanks Giving

Ron Shaw

Chapter 1. Yes or No

In ten days, Thanksgiving 2016 would be a wrap.

For one metro Atlanta family, this meant two of three sisters had less than a day to decide whether or not to be at their parent's table for the feast. The oldest sister, Glenda, would be there, showcasing her new love interest. Her younger sisters, Cindy and Ricki, wanted no part of the brewing disaster.

"Tom, do you want to go or not?" Tom's wife Cindy of thirty years and mother of their two children, Will and Bethany, blurted out while the morning coffee percolated.

Dropping two sugar cubes into his waiting cup, her usually obedient husband, Tom, answered, "Go where? What time is it? When will that coffee be ready? ... Where?"

Bringing the pot to his cup, his wife replied, "You know what I'm asking... Thanksgiving."

"Oh, we're on the Thanksgiving thing again. I told you I'd do what you decided. I'll go if you want. The kids are looking forward to the festive madness."

"Whose kids, Tom?"

"Yours, dear," Cindy's husband said, stirring his first cup of java.

"When did this happen? The last I heard Bethany was spending the holiday with her boyfriend's family in Denver, and Will was off to Utah, skiing with his UGA frat friends."

"Oops, honey, I forgot to tell you. The kids phoned earlier this week while you were either at the mall or your doctor's appointment. Bethany and her boyfriend are history, and Will can't ski anyway. They loved the idea of potentially seeing the ambulance, fire engines, and police again at your Mom and Dad's house. They'll be home in a few days."

"You forgot?" his suddenly irritated wife retorted.

"Yep, sorry. I'm just a fallible human being, I suppose," he stated before laughing after taking a sip of steaming hot liquid.

"Tom, now we have to attend. The good Lord only knows what'll happen this year. I didn't want to go. Have you forgotten the last Thanksgiving at Mom's?"

"Certainly not. It has only been five years, and the whole thing was a blast. It was the best Turkey Day ever," grinning with eyes twinkling, Tom said.

"No wonder our children would rather talk with you than me. They're just like you. It was a disaster. We ended up eating at a Huddle House."

"Cindy, it wasn't so bad. My steak was good, and the hospital was like a party. The doctor and nurses enjoyed it. There's hardly any scarring on your arm from those stitches. Your sister, Ricki, needs to manage her meds better this time or another ambulance will come screaming."

"Enough already. I don't wish to relive it. Why didn't you tell me Bethany was single again? He was a nice young man. What happened?"

"Hold on. Our son and daughter helped put out the fire, too," walking over to his wife with empty cup in hand, Tom added, hugging his worried wife.

"I remember it all, Tom. Get on with the Bethany information."

"Don't quote me on this, but Bethany said her beau was caught dipping his device in a newer, evenly-tanned server — a dark-haired, buxom senior from Hollywood. I think she's a 'Ramblin' Wreck from Georgia Tech' cheerleader."

"Oh my goodness! Who caught him?"

"Dear, pour me another cup. Your daughter walked in on them, doing the dirty deed, and she kicked his ass. Those are her words, not mine. He's toast. I never liked Blane anyway. Georgia Tech has too many California, surfer dudes going there. Who on God's blue planet names their son Blane?"

Changing the subject, spreading homemade strawberry jam on her wheat toast, Cindy inquired, "Our children will be home in a couple of days?"

"Yep, in just two days from yesterday or so. We'll probably see them today or tomorrow," Tom responded, stating "Oops" under his coffee-warmed breath.

"The three of you will be the death of me. Alright, no problem. It'll be great having them home for the holiday. I have to convince sister Ricki and her family to join us at Mom's and Dad's. She and I do want to meet sister Glenda's new love, and it'd be nice to see their twins. Our nieces are studying at Southern Cal, you know."

"I am familiar, but wait a second. Did you say Glenda has a new love, and why do you always refer to them as sister before stating their names?" he inquired, lazily thumbing through the morning paper.

"What do you mean? I don't *always* do it. Sometimes, I do. It's what we were raised to do. You know our parents used to call us simply sister. We added the names later because sometimes, it was confusing even to us. You're totally correct. Glenda does have a new love."

"What happened to the gorgeous and delicious Ms. college professor? She was fantastic," Tom commented, glancing over the top of his paper, winking at his wife.

"She wasn't close to your description, and stop the winking-eye thing," turning her back to her husband, she giggled slightly.

"Cindy, I thought so. She was beautiful, intelligent, witty, and outgoing."

"What is it about some men and lesbians? Please, explain it to me, if you can... and be careful."

Dropping the newspaper to the table's surface, he replied, "Well, this is an easy one. We, hetero guys, share something in common with them, and for me, it's a matter of anyone being a decent, friendly, interesting, and caring person. The college professor was all of these, and hopefully, she remains so. Plus, I find it both beneficial and easy to appreciate beauty in women — like you, my only and dearest."

"I understand. You're right. I'll agree this time only, it is simple, but don't think for a second you've escaped the hook with me."

"Why did they split?" Tom probed, frowning while feeling the barb of his wife's stare.

"It seems your daughter's ex-boyfriend and the dish of a professor had a few things in common."

"Do tell," Tom responded, forgetting about the hook and dog's house for a brief moment.

"A month or so ago, Glenda returned home a day early from a business trip, catching her partner in their bed with one of her blonde, buxom, graduate students."

"Oh, I see — working out her 'A', huh?"

"Exactly, but this dalliance earned the professor a swift 'B-B' as in Bye-Bye from Glenda."

"Who's Glenda seeing now?"

"All I've learned about her is they've known each other for years through work, and she's almost half Glenda's age."

"Speaking of me on the hook alone, you tell me what it is about some women who go after lovers half their age?"

"I think they share something with many men."

"Touché. I'm feeling the pain from your fishing gear again."

"Tomorrow afternoon, I'll advise Mom we'll be there... the four of us. I have tonight and tomorrow morning to convince Ricki to attend. Mom has us scheduled tomorrow at 1 PM for a four-way conference call with her. Can you believe it? Mom can barely sign on with the laptop computer we gifted her last Christmas, but she has a conference telephone line."

"Nope, it sounds wild to me. Hey, you may want to have your sisters on the line thirty minutes or so earlier with you before your Mom pops in. You can do it. I'm sure you'll have things to discuss among the three of you," Tom offered, heading for their fridge and a sweet cantaloupe.

"Honey, it's a great idea. I'll also call Glenda this evening. Did you bring the trash receptacle back from the curb?" she asked, handing him a bowl for his fruit. "On to other things," she said.

"How pretty is she?" Tom wondered, hoping to hear more about Glenda's new lover.

"Who?"

"Her new girlfriend."

"How about the garbage receptacle?" she quipped, tossing the paper back on the table.

"I'll do it in a minute."

"In a minute, in a minute, you and Dad could be cloned twins. I've heard you two say this thousands of times. Yours and his 'in-a-minutes' never come."

"Hey, yes they do, eventually, but don't blame me. Your Dad schooled me on this tactic years ago. We can't cave immediately on the things y'all tell us to do. If we did, there'd be no free minute left for our goofing off. Often we eventually do it," he answered, heading at a rotund snail's pace towards their kitchen door.

"Ha- ha, you're so funny. Fetch the emptied can."

"After you answer my question, I'll go."

"What question?"

"Is she pretty?"

"Have you ever known Glenda to have a love interest who wasn't beautiful?"

Making it to the kitchen door, Tom answered, "Good point," as he headed for the driveway despite the frigid air of November lying in wait.

Chapter 2. The Call

Cindy made the evening phone calls to her sisters, Ricki and Glenda, comparing notes on their strategy for the impending conference call with Mom and their soon approaching family debacle, Thanksgiving.

It was easy to talk Ricki into joining the family once she'd heard her sisters and their loved ones were attending. Like Cindy and Tom's children, it seems the twins were eager to see what would happen this year at Grandma's house. The identical twins loved their Grandparents on both sides, but their Mom's parents were even more special to them because they were a tad and a half quirky as their Mom and her sisters used to suggest.

Like their mother, both USC Trojans were well beyond attractive. They were the kind of young ladies who could momentarily stop a young boy's heart at first sight from fifty yards away.

They'd received athletic scholarships to the University of Southern California. Ivy was a cheerleader and Rose a tennis player. The only physical difference between the two was their muscular development. Rose had the long and slightly-chiseled arms and muscular thighs of a tennis player. Ivy's body was more lean and angular like you'd expect of an Olympic swimmer.

One by one, the three sisters dialed into the conference "room." They were there at 12:30 PM. Their Mom would join them at least by 1 PM, but they knew she'd be a little early.

Cindy was always the most sensible of the three, leading their conversation. Glenda and Ricki were comfortable with this. Unlike Cindy, their personalities were closer to those of their Mom and Dad. Glenda was like her Dad and Ricki her Mom.

Taking the lead, Cindy said, "I have a head count of twelve for Thanksgiving," followed by, "Does this sound correct to you guys?"

Ricki responded, "Did you add Aunt Edna? Mom told me weeks ago she was a sure thing."

Jumping in, Glenda added, "Ricki's right. Mom gave me the same information. This would make it thirteen."

"Oh crap! Thirteen is an omen of bad things to come. I knew it. This year is doomed already," Cindy whined, knowing their children would receive what they joyfully wanted.

Glenda, the oldest, stated with confidence, "Cut it out Miss 'Constant-Gloomy-and-Doomy.' You're always thinking the worst. Everything's going to be fine. Thirteen is just a stupid number, nothing more. Hold on and let me do a recount. You might be wrong, Cindy."

"No. I'm right. Ricki's clan plus my family makes eight, plus you and your date makes ten, add Mom and Dad, making it twelve and Aunt Edna tops the list off at thirteen. This stinks."

"Cindy, calm down. I'm with Glenda. Who cares about a silly number? How bad can it be? We did it all last time, and lightning never strikes the same place twice."

"Look who's spouting superstition now. Alright, I'll drop it, but remember who said it. Something has to give or tragedy will strike a second time. Ricki, you better stay out of the Emergency Room this go around. For goodness sake, don't over-medicate because of the pressure," Cindy directed, raising her voice for the last comment.

"Girl, please, look who's talking. You beat me to the Eastside Hospital Emergency Room by fifteen minutes by slicing your arm open," Ricky responded, preparing for another skirmish of words.

"The cut was an accident, and you guys know it, Cindy retorted. "Mom had sent me to my house for a few extra folding chairs. This is great. Hold it against me because I live only a couple of miles from Mom and Dad. My attic was dark. The chairs were stored there. Looking for the light switch, I stumbled, cutting my arm on the broken light shade," explaining for what seemed like the fifteenth time.

"You babies knock it off. That was five years ago. We'll be fine as long as Mom and Dad don't try burning their house down again," showing her usual lack of patience, in disgust, Glenda stated and continued, "This brings a question to mind. Please, Cindy or Ricki, tell me Mom isn't insisting on Dad deep-frying the turkey inside the kitchen this year?"

"I covered this dangerous one with her weeks ago. She assured me she wouldn't think of embarrassing themselves in front of Lisa, and there'd be no frying of a large bird in the house. She's baking a twenty-five pounder," Cindy said, exhaling a huge breath of relief.

Giggling like they were teens again, Ricki said, "Cindy, you know Mom had bought Dad the new, large, electric fryer, insisting he cook the turkey in the kitchen. Dad didn't want to, but we know Mom."

"Oh, I recall, Ricki. They should've known better. But Mom did get a new kitchen out of the mess," Cindy answered, chuckling with her younger sister.

Almost in a laugh, Glenda added, "Do you remember what Aunt Edna did while the countertops were burning?"

"I so do," Cindy said, laughing loudly now, trying to answer her sister. "Her hair was smoking as she bent over and lit a cigarette from the fire, calling Dad a jackass while the kids took charge. Mom was running around screaming with her arms flailing. Dad was in the corner, covered in soot, howling his fool head off at Aunt Edna and the roaring fire."

"Sadly, you're right. Luckily, the turkey exploded skyward to the ceiling. Parts were embedded in the sheetrock. It was surreal like a Salvador Dali painting," Glenda added, chuckling with her sisters.

None of the daughters had heard their Mother's bell ring when she had entered the call.

"What are you geese cackling about?" Mom interrupted, in a serious tone they knew all too well.

Straightening up first, sitting erect in her chair, Cindy answered, "Nothing much, Mom. We're telling stories."

"I have things to do. So y'all quiet down. Is everybody in for Thanksgiving... I'm hoping my grandchildren, too?"

Quickly, feeling guilty, the three girls answered, "Yes."

"That's excellent. It's going to be a traditional meal. Y'all are familiar with the menu. We plan on eating at noon, but you know this means sometime before one, I hope. Don't bring a thing, and do not make it a point to arrive too early. I plan on getting lots of work out of the old man. If you arrive too soon, he'll disappear. Y'all know this. I'm serious. Bring nothing except your appetites. I have it all under control. Your Aunt Edna's bringing the liquor. Since the kids are older, I assume we'll have thirteen eating and drinking Edna's booze. Your father and I can't wait to see those college kids and to finally meet your new friend, Glenda."

Slicing the momentary silence, Glenda answered first, "Thanks, Mom. We'll be there."

"Mom, you've promised us, no deep-frying," quipped Cindy, as serious as a pastor on Sunday.

"No way. Not this year. I love my new kitchen, and that old man won't deep-fry this one."

Jumping into the conversation, Ricki offered, "Mom, your kitchen isn't new. It's been five years now since the fire. Are you certain we can't bring anything?"

"I insist — not a single thing. Now, we've cackled enough. I have to go. I'm meeting Edna in Buckhead, Atlanta for drinks and a bite at two. Your Dad and I dine out so much these days, this kitchen still feels new to me. I'll see you all Thanksgiving Day. Goodbye, girls."

Before her daughters replied in unison, "Bye, Mom," Glenda reminded her Buckhead was simply a section within the northern part of Atlanta and not a city proper.

The conference call ended.

Chapter 3. Edna

The tension at Cindy's house was building. Thanksgiving was three days away, and their children were home for the break.

"Will, what happened with your skiing trip?"

"Mom, I really didn't want to go, breaking a leg or arm doesn't appeal to me. I'm having so much fun at Georgia, hobbling around campus would be a complete drag," her son answered, munching Cheetos between sentences.

"Danged, brother, close your mouth while you eat. He's having fun alright, staying wasted day and night, I'll wager," Bethany responded, smacking her fresh ball of chewing gum.

"You've got lots of room to talk, sis, chomping on your bubble gum. I've heard about those 'Killer Bees and Hot Honeys' parties at Georgia Tech."

"You know nothing, fledgling freshman. We have to earn our degrees at Tech."

"Right. I forgot you'll soon be a 'helluva, helluva engineer' and all the other crap because you're a Ramblin' Wreck from Georgia Tech. We're kicking your asses between the hedges this year."

"Woof, woof, woof, baby Bulldog brother."

"Y'all stop it. You're giving me a migraine. You better clean your language up while you're at it. We pay too much money for you two to use profanity so cavalierly."

"Okay, Mom, I'll stop if he does."

"You have a deal, big sis."

"Mom, what'll be on the table at Grandma's? I think we can allow Bethany to eat at the big table this year," stated Will, while poking his sister gently in the ribs.

"I said enough, you too. Stop hitting your sister, Will. Your Grandmother said it'll be her traditional menu. But to refresh your memories, knowing how clouded your brains are from your studies, there'll be baked turkey, homemade turkey gravy, dressing, not stuffing, whipped potatoes, creamed corn, green bean casserole, English peas, sweet potato soufflé, stuffed celery stalks, stuffed deviled eggs with olives on top, jellied cranberry sauce, brown and serve rolls, sweetened iced tea, and coffee. Knowing Mom, she'll also have a baked ham. For dessert, we can expect pumpkin and pecan pies and a homemade cake, either chocolate icing on yellow cake or a coconut cake. But, if your Grandfather has his way, it'll be a devil's food cake with white icing."

"I love Grandma's cooking." Will licked his orange stained lips.

"Me, too, little brother," Bethany responded, filling a glass with chilled grapefruit juice, commencing work on taking a pound or two off before turkey day..

"Mom has always been an excellent cook, but you know your Grandpa does about seventy percent of it all at her orders. He's already busy shopping, preparing, cutting, and dicing like one of those sous chefs on the food channel. This is the main reason Mom doesn't want us to arrive too early. We'll see how much of the work 'the old man', as she calls him, is really doing. She's the maestro, and he better hit the right notes when she's conducting her masterpiece," Cindy said, laughing at Bethany's facial contortions at drinking straight grapefruit juice.

Opting for a cold Pepsi from their fridge, Will added, "It's a kick to listen to them go at each other. Grandpa will suffer enough of it and disappear. He's taken me outside with him or to a store plenty of times to escape for a few minutes. He's a funny man."

"I know, son. He and she have done these type of things our entire lives. They love each other dearly, and they've figured out what works for them and their relationship. It's a comforting and beautiful thing to watch."

"Yep, like you and Dad, Mom. Y'all are a lot like them."

"I know we are, Will. Your father married well."

Giggling, Bethany responded, "And so we hear precisely what Dad would say about you. Is Aunt Edna coming this year?"

"She is, Bethany."

After a loud belch, Will asked, "How old is she now?"

"I believe she turned seventy-seven or eight in October. She was born on Halloween night, and she's been tricking and treating us since I was a little girl. God sent her into the world on the perfect date."

"She doesn't look a day over a hundred and two."

"Stop it, Will, and quit belching on purpose. She's a darling."

"Mom, she's three full loads of fun, but she's also sort of crazy."

"Bethany, she is what she is, and we adore her, always have."

"I understand, Mom, and Will and I do also, but she's still a ton of zany plus fun. For example, reportedly, she's never been married and brags about it. I've not heard her speak of an old beau or anyone close to being one. She drinks like five fish on shore leave, smoking skinny cigarettes like a bonfire. She wears designer clothes and continues to work in the ladies lingerie department of a department store in downtown Atlanta. Aunt Edna drives a 1967 Fastback Mustang. Like her face sometimes, her car is candy-apple red, and she swears like a pro."

"Hell yes! These are all the reasons why she's so neat, sis. I have a ball talking with her. She is the life of any party. Just wait until Thursday. Aunt Edna will waltz in late like a tipsy movie star, dazzling all of us with her dry wit and intelligence. I can barely wait to see her smoke-filled entrance. Mom, who else is coming?"

"Your Aunt Ricki, Uncle Bill, the twins, Aunt Glenda, and her date will join us, making the total thirteen with Aunt Edna."

"Who's Aunt Glenda's date? Is she still living with the Georgia State University professor? I think she taught English."

"No, Bethany, she isn't, and I don't wish to discuss it."

"Why not? College campuses have plenty of lesbians and homosexual men on them. Including high school, Will and I have had a good many gay friends. Still do. It's no big thing these days. It's just normal, Mom," Bethany explained with authority, placing her empty glass in the dishwasher.

"I know it is, honey, but couples breaking up like you and Blane and your Aunt Glenda's recent partner problems bothers me deeply. It's not a matter of sexual preference or gender. It saddens me... this is all I'm attempting to convey. Her new love interest is Lisa, but be prepared because we hear she's not much older than you, Bethany."

"Alright, Aunt Glenda scores!"

"Will, you're crass. Grow up."

"Sis, put a sock in it. Aunt Glenda's cool like Aunt Edna."

"Enough already, we've exhausted the subject. Both of you, out of here. Go shopping or something. Be home for dinner. Your Dad needs to spend some quality time with you clowns."

"I'm driving Aunt Edna's Mustang this year, wait and see."

"Close your big pie hole, Georgia Bulldog clown, and let's go to the mall."

"I'm driving."

"No, you're not, too-scared-to-ski boy."

"Will, your sister's driving. Bye and go."

"Later, Mom," Bethany said, throwing her hand up, waving while exiting the kitchen door.

"Bye, Mother dearest," Will said, kissing his mom on her right cheek.

"Have fun, y'all."

Chapter 4. The Dreaded List

"Quincy, here's your list for the next three days," the old man's wife, Vera, announced.

Cringing at the mere thought of his Thanksgiving "honey-do" list, Quincy retorted, "There better not be more than fifty items on your paper. I won't do one thing over fifty. I mean it, Vera. The last time we did this you had written down sixty-five orders for me. My back can't take it this year. I'm telling you."

"Stop your griping. There's only forty-two on it, and the first half of them are the groceries you need to buy today," she responded by erasing a couple of things from his list.

"Forty-two sounds more like it. I can handle those as long as you let me do them at my own pace. We've done this so many times over the past fifty years, I could make short work of the list in my sleep," Quincy bragged, feeling vindicated.

"Right. You keep thinking like it's easy. If I don't stay on you, you'll mess up at least ten of the things we must have."

"Give me the blasted list. I'm on the way to the grocery store. I'll be back when you see me." Exiting the kitchen with paper in hand, Quincy hurried to escape further orders, mumbling a few choice complaints under his breath.

Shouting from the kitchen, Vera yelped, "Take the frozen turkey from the freezer and put it in the refrigerator out there in the garage. It'll take close to three days for it to thaw." A minute or so later, Vera heard their car door slam shut without comment from Quincy.

The grocery list was crossed off, and the feisty old man was proud of himself, knowing he'd bought all she'd requested. There were twenty tasks to go with plenty of work for them to do before the big feast.

Those who've never prepared such an elaborate meal for a crowd of people have no idea what the task entails. There's at least two days of prep work to accomplish in order to have things lined up so the meal can come together in a synchronized and timely manner. For the devoted couple, many years of performing this culinary symphony didn't negate the tedious, labor-intensive, and time-consuming work.

Quincy went about crossing things off his list under the constant scrutiny of the head chef, Vera.

By Thanksgiving eve, all was sitting on ready for the next morning's final act. The plump turkey would have to be seasoned and placed in the oven by no later than 7:30 AM on Thanksgiving Day. It would take between four and five hours to properly cook. The dressing, sweet potato soufflé, mashed potatoes, gravy, and other vegetables would be cooked when their bird was removed from the oven so they'd be piping hot when the dinner bell rang. The cranberry sauce, stuffed deviled eggs, stuffed celery, cold beverage, and desserts were prepared in advance, refrigerated and waiting. The buttered rolls would be last in the oven. The coffee would be made fresh on an as-needed basis throughout feast day.

Their dining room table with seasonal centerpiece would be fully set, waiting and ready for the hungry crowd.

Chapter 5. Willard's Mission

The twenty-four miles from Quincy and Vera's home to downtown Atlanta was a universe away as it would concern a homeless drunk named Willard Jones.

All holidays were painful for Willard, a saltine cracker-thin man with a ruddy freckled complexion almost the same color as a three-day-old cadaver. Living from inside one cheap wine bottle to the next, the decades had eaten away at his soul. His embattled teeth showed the signs of the assault. There was but a flicker of life left in his emaciated body, riddled from years of malnutrition, accompanying his alcohol abuse. He was the kind of man who preferred killing himself, swilling one ounce at a time. His life sentence of dying daily had been self-imposed.

Almost innately, two days before Thanksgiving 2016, crawling from beneath the shrubbery he had called bed the night before, Willard began his yearly walk to Snellville, Georgia. With a little luck, he'd be half sober by the time he reached the Decatur City Limits... better luck still, snatched from his miserable life for his unforgivable sins before entering Snellville.

If a little luck prevailed, by Thanksgiving, he'd be home with loved ones again. Each year, it was the sole day he would attempt to face sober. Often, he had failed.

Chapter 6. Turkey for None

On Turkey Day, Quincy was up by 5:30 AM, working on his meal duties with a large coffee in hand. Entering the kitchen several minutes later, Vera took charge.

"Let's prepare the turkey for the oven. Fetch it from the fridge, get it washed, clean it out, and I'll season it. I'd rather it be ready a little early than late," Vera directed, fetching the spices and herbs for the bird.

Without hesitation, Quincy grabbed the frozen turkey, plopping it on the counter next to the sink.

"Old man, this bird better not be frozen. The thud sounded frozen. Didn't you place it in the garage refrigerator like I instructed? You recall me telling to do so when you went grocery shopping, right?" his irritated wife stated.

"What, I didn't hear..." stammering he tried to explain before being interrupted.

"Oh, no, you didn't. You realize this turkey can't be cooked frozen, and you know I told you."

"Nope, I didn't hear it, and it wasn't on my list. Look. Here's my list. It's not on there."

"Old man, I swear. Is it totally frozen?"

"Yep, solid as your diamond wedding ring," Quincy replied, holding his laughter for his immediate safety.

"Be quiet for a minute, let me think. If we don't get this bird thawed in an hour there'll be no turkey and no meat today. Old man, do what I say and make it quick."

Quincy saw red in her eyes, knowing better than to say a word. It was time to act or be brained with a frozen twenty-five pounder.

"Okay, unwrap it, get it washed. I'll be back in a minute. Have it ready," Vera barked, darting from the kitchen after her last order.

In two minutes, she returned, carrying a folded, clean, large, pillow case.

The wet bird and Quincy were waiting.

"Take some paper towels and dab it dry, all over now."

He did.

Vera opened the pillow case. "Put it inside," she stated, breathing heavily.

It was done.

"Take it to the laundry room, close the case top, use a bag tie, and pop it inside the dryer. Set the timer for an hour and hit dry. Hurry, old man. If we're living right, it'll be thawed in an hour. We can have it in the oven by 7 or 7:30 at the latest."

Quincy hopped to with a newly born quickness and a look of urgency consuming his face.

Exiting the laundry room, the loud banging from the bird tumbling in the dryer sent Vera into another panic.

The old man knew better than to laugh.

"Quickly, run to the bathroom closet and grab a big armful of clean bath towels... better yet, bring the beach towels. We'll place them in with the bird. Hopefully, they'll cushion it, ending the noise. We don't want to bruise the meat. My hands are covered in sweet potatoes. Before you fetch the towels, stop the dryer."

He did as told, placing the towels in with the turkey, hitting the dry button a second time. This solved this problem.

In all, it stayed in the dryer for eighty minutes. The hot bird was brought into the kitchen where the pillow case was opened.

"What did you do?" Vera inquired, holding a large butcher's knife in her hand.

"What?"

"This turkey smells like lilacs. Don't tell me — please, don't say you put one of the lilac dryer sheets inside the pillow case."

"Okay. I won't say it. But you might find two in there."

"Oh, my heavens, you did," Vera grunted, pulling the spent fragranced sheet from the case.

"Sometimes, I don't know what to do with you. Why in creation did you do that?"

"Hey, each time I do the drying, and if I forget to add one, you jump on me. So, I figured, what the hell."

"Rinse it off thoroughly, and let's see if we can wash away some of the sweet odor. DO NOT use soap."

"Dang. Alright. I think it smells really good, like fresh lilacs."

Quincy did as best he could without telling her he'd also left the packaged innards and severed neck inside the frozen bird. He figured she'd smack him if anything else he'd done was wrong.

"I'll try to tone down the lilacs with extra seasonings. Place it in the pan, fold its wings under its chest, and add about an inch of water to the pan. Put six cubes of chicken bouillon into the water around the bird. Please, for goodness sake, remove the wrapping from the cubes first," beyond annoyed with her husband, she advised.

Vera did her seasoning thing.

Gently, Quincy placed it into the hot oven. It was time to broil the skin for a few minutes to attain the perfect golden coloration from baking. This was done.

The oven was placed on bake at 375 degrees. Once the broiling element went off, a meat thermometer was inserted into the breast closest to the oven door.

"It should be ready by noon," Vera stated, exhaling a sigh of relief.

Within an hour, their brick ranch was filled with a hybrid aroma of roasting turkey and sweet lilacs.

Quincy quipped, "Old woman, your bird smells better than any we've cooked."

"Don't push me, old man. Where'd you put the rolls?"

"What rolls?"

"The ones you bought at the store. The dozen brown and serve ones and eighteen French rolls for today's meal. The ones on your list."

"My list didn't have rolls on it."

"Hand it over," she demanded, turning red-faced at the thought of another screw-up by Quincy.

He did.

"I'll be. You're right. I forget to put the rolls on it. Go find some."

"What? Find rolls today? Are you completely insane? It's Thanksgiving Day, old woman."

"Yes. We have to have rolls with the meal."

"What's wrong with loaf bread? They might want a turkey sandwich anyway."

"Old man!"

"Alright. I'll go in a minute. My back's killing me."

"You'll go right now or you won't need your back."

"Where am I going to find rolls?"

"I'd try Walmart first. I think I read somewhere they'd be open today at ten."

"If they open at ten, I'll wait for Will to arrive and take him with me. You know Cindy always comes earlier than anyone else."

"Sounds good to me, as long as you find rolls. They'll be here well before eleven.

"Go rest your back for a while. I've got things under control in the kitchen. Put your heating pad on it — watch the parade. You and Will can fetch them in plenty of time."

Winking at his wife and smiling, her old man headed for his den recliner, rubbing an aching back.

Chapter 7. Plus One

Will and his family made it to their Grandparent's house before eleven. They lived a couple of miles away. After hugs and greetings, Grandpa culled Will from the bunch for the trip in search of rolls.

Concerned and suspicious, Cindy stated, "Mom, where are Will and Dad going?"

"Your father forgot to buy the rolls. They're going to Walmart."

"Mom, I have rolls. I brought three packages of the ones we like. Didn't Tom bring them in? Bethany, go out and see if your dad left the bag of rolls in the vehicle."

"Okay, Mom," Bethany answered, delighted to leave the humid kitchen for a few minutes.

"What are we going to do with these men, Mom?" Cindy said, opening the oven to have a better look at the turkey.

"Honey, after fifty years with your Father, do you really think I have a clue?"

Bethany returned with the rolls.

"It'll be alright, Cindy. The chore will give Will and your Dad a chance to bond a little, hopefully, not too much, though. Your father will corrupt the boy."

"I know. Like he did Tom," Cindy replied, raising her right eyebrow, tilting her head slightly to the left.

"You're right," Vera answered, laughing with her daughter.

Quincy was in no hurry to make it to Walmart.

"Will, how's school?"

"It's great, Grandpa. Everywhere you look there are beautiful girls. The parties are unbelievable."

"Son, you can either party or get an education. You have a lifetime to party. Concentrate on your studies. You'll eventually learn how to have them both, but don't burn yourself out."

"I don't. I'm earning good grades, making all of my classes and assignments," Will answered, wrestling with a tight wrapper on a stick of gum.

"Son, we're proud of you and Bethany. Reach inside the glove box, way down at the bottom, and hand me the bottle of whiskey. It's quite nippy out this morning. A quick snort will warm us up."

"Here you go, Grandpa."

"You first, Will. It's good sipping whiskey. Take a slug and get yourself warm before the heater cranks up."

Will took a small draw from the bottle, shaking as the liquid slid down his throat.

"Smooth, eh? I told you. This is the good stuff. It warmed you up. Didn't it?"

"It sure did," Will returned, chomping on his peppermint gum.

"One nip is all we need. Put it back in the glove box under those papers. We don't want Vera or anyone else finding it too easily."

The customer parking lot of the Snellville Walmart was ten cars shy of being barren, but it was open for business.

Quincy parked in his usual space under the outstretched limbs of a small tree, resting on an island near the only side entrance of the store.

Today was different, though. Half-reclining beneath the tree on the grass was a skinny man, teetering on

126

his lap was a half-swilled, large bottle of cheap wine. By all appearances, he seemed to be intoxicated, sleeping off a doozy, if the store's few customers were lucky.

Firmly shutting his car door, Will woke the dirty drunk who immediately asked the boy for a dollar.

"Son, we generally don't see this in Snellville. We're usually wino free. Here, Will, take this money, go inside, and buy the rolls. You know the ones we like. Get two packs, a pack of a dozen brown and serve, and one of those French kind also for baking. The French ones will have more rolls inside. If they're out of either of them double up on the style they do have. I'll be with you in a minute. I want to check on this guy. He looks familiar to me. I may have seen him in Atlanta or something. I'll at least give him a little money," Quincy advised, keeping a keen eye on the inebriated panhandler.

Will proceeded into the store.

"Sir, can I help you? Are you alright?" Quincy said, leaning over closer to the man.

"Loan me a dollar," he responded, outstretching a filthy hand.

"Here are a few bucks for you. Can I take you somewhere? Do you have family in Snellville?"

"Sure, across the street," the intoxicated man replied, pointing towards a church and graveyard.

"Which street?" Quincy said, confused by the cryptic response of the bum.

"This road. Are you drinking, too?" the unshaven man stated, gulping a big swallow of wine. Obviously, the drunk wasn't as inebriated as the bottle would indicate.

"Sir, I'm Quincy Johns. You look familiar to me. Do we know each other?"

The wino looked up, staring from beneath his soiled, Georgia Tech, baseball cap. "I don't know. My name's Willard. Folks used to call me Willie."

"I'll be damned, Willie. We went to Roosevelt High School in Atlanta together. I sat near you in many classes because of our last names, Johns and Jones."

"Hey, you're right. I remember you, too. They called you Quince. I never did, but some of them did."

"Correct, Willard. Do you have anywhere to go? Can I drive you home or wherever?"

"I don't own a home any more. I'm where I need to be," Willie answered, taking a smaller slug of alcohol.

"When's the last time you had a hot meal?"

"Been a while, mister."

"Would you do me an honor and celebrate Thanksgiving with me and my family? I live about three miles from here. Afterwards, I'll take you anywhere you want to go," Quincy offered, extending a hand to help the man up, hopefully.

"Can you drive me back to Atlanta?"

"Certainly. No problem. After we eat and chat a little, I'll bring you to Atlanta."

"Okay. Thank you, Quincy."

"It's my pleasure, Willard. Let me help you into my car."

"I can make it. I'm not too drunk. It was a long walk from Atlanta. I was tired. Have a sip of wine with me," Willard said, handing the bottle over to Quincy.

"Don't mind if I do. Thanks, Willie."

Quincy took a respectable drink from the bottle, helping his old classmate into the car.

Will exited the store, carrying a bag filled with rolls.

Climbing into the back seat, Will didn't say a word. The three of them remained silent on the drive back to the Johns' residence.

Apparently, while they were away, all of their guests had arrived.

Quincy figured this "plus one" would be a difficult one to sell to his wife and a few of his other family members. Already worried, a superstitious Cindy would embrace the new number... now, fourteen for dinner.

Chapter 8. Black Coffee and a Bath

Leaving the wine bottle in the car, the men entered the house with bread in hand.

"Honey, we have one more for dinner. I'd like for you to meet a Roosevelt schoolmate of mine. This is Willard Jones. Willard this is my wife, Vera."

"Pleased to make your acquaintance, ma'am. Your house is lovely. Something sure smells great. I love the fragrance of lilacs. Pardon my appearance. Thank you for having me."

They shook hands.

"It's nice to meet you, Willard. This is our family. Guys come over and introduce yourselves to Mr. Jones," Vera announced, backing away from the stench coming from Willard.

One by one, each person did as Vera had requested, giving her the ideal opportunity to interrogate Quincy alone about this stranger.

"Old man, have you lost your mind? Who is this man? He stinks like rotten booze, and he's filthy. What do you have to say for yourself?"

"Vera, he's our guest. He needs our help. Giving is what this day is about. My head's in the right place. You need to check yours. This is final," Quincy said with utmost resolve.

"I'm sorry, honey. Of course, you're right. Give him plenty of black coffee. Take him back to our bedroom. Find him some clean clothes, shoes, and all, and start a bath for him. We'll delay lunch a few minutes while he gets ready."

"There's the spirit. Hey, his aroma has muted the lilacs a little."

"I know. Thank God for small favors. Everyone has been laughing about the aroma. I didn't tell them what we did. I said it was a new secret ingredient. They like the fragrance."

Quincy assisted Willard as Vera had suggested.

Within thirty minutes, a sober, clean-shaven, handsome stranger joined the family in the den. Willard Jones' physical transformation was breathtaking to Edna. She demanded he be seated next to her at the table. Vera arranged it, knowing something was brewing between Edna and Willard. Their flirting and glancing looks at each other were obvious to Vera and Quincy.

The same could be said about sister Glenda and her new love, Lisa.

Chapter 9. Let's Eat

Quincy announced, "Let's eat, gang. I'm famished."

The family filed into the dining room, taking their seats. The table was flush with food from end to end. In front of Quincy, the turkey rested, glowing golden with a light purple glaze. He'd carve the bird for the family. This was their tradition. He would be the last to sit and lift fork to mouth, and he wouldn't have it any other way.

The sisters and grandkids chattered while the carving took place, passing of bowls and trays of food around the table occurred simultaneously.

Lisa was getting on marvelously with Glenda's family.

Edna and Willard whispered, moving closer to each other.

"Lisa, thank you for bringing the baked ham. You didn't have to bring anything but an appetite," Vera stated, welcoming Lisa to their table and family.

"It was no trouble, Mrs. Johns. There's a Honey-Baked Hams store a block from my flat. I wanted to do something."

"Well, we appreciate it, dear and call me Vera. It looks lovely. Their hams are always cooked perfectly. If you wouldn't mind, tell us a little about yourself?"

"I'd love to, Vera. Let me see, where should I start? I'm older than I look. Let me admit I have forty years in my rearview mirror. Many people think I'm in my early thirties, and I love it. I'm an Atlanta native, owning a flat in the refurbished, Fulton Bag Mill complex. I have a PhD in English Literature from Emory University, and I've worked for Glenda's publishing company for fifteen years. I'm the projects' manager there. Glenda and I have been friends since we first met. I was always romantically interested in her, but for years, I kept it a secret. As much as it sounds pushy, after she broke it off with her last partner, I told her of my feelings towards her, and here we are. This is about it."

"Thanks for sharing, Lisa. You're lovely," Vera responded, dipping a pinch of roll into a small pool of gravy on her plate.

Paying no attention to Lisa's comments, the twins, Ivy and Rose giggled, telling and comparing tall tales of college with Bethany and Will.

His doting daughter Ricki had made her dad a devil's food cake with white icing. Before they had taken their seats at the table, Vera had to threaten him two times when his cutting knife was approaching the fluffy icing. Will saw to it Grandpa had a small slice before the table was readied.

The choice of white or dark meat was distributed per each person's preference. Like his Grandpa, Will wanted both.

Quincy took his seat.

"Aunt Edna, will you say the prayer for us?" This was also a family tradition. The eldest at the table did so.

"Certainly, Quincy. Bow your heads please, " she began and all complied.

"Father, we appreciate this day of thanks and giving. Bless this family. Thank you for these new friends, Lisa and Willard. In your infinite wisdom, you've led them here to us on this special occasion. Thank you for our hosts, Vera and Quincy, and thank you for this fine food. May it nourish our bodies as you nourish our souls. In your name, we pray, Amen."

"Let's eat!" Quincy proclaimed, forking his initial bite of Lisa's baked ham.

Chapter 10. Dessert Is Served

It didn't take long for all fourteen to finish their meal. During it, the chatter was nonstop with periods of laughter, echoing throughout the house.

Like a military leader after a victorious battle, Vera announced, "Lisa, Edna, Willard, and kids, y'all sit tight and talk. The rest of you help me clear the table of the food and dirty dishes. Ricki and Glenda, place the dirty dishes in the sink. I'll make your Dad take care of them later. Cindy, you and I will put all the food up. Men, while we're getting this done, bring the desserts and plates from the kitchen table into the dining room, placing them on the table. Make sure you set the old man's devil's food cake in front of him. Tom and Bill, ask who wants coffee, milk, or tea and serve it to them, please. Old man, I see someone has eaten a piece of this cake. Will, you're in trouble with your Grandfather."

"Son, pay your Grandma no attention. I'll handle her," Quincy proclaimed, eyeing a big slice of cake waiting on his fork.

"Grandpa, how does she see every little thing? Her back was to me the entire time I did it."

"Will, my old woman has eyes and ears in the back of her head. She's like a bat with radar," Quincy proclaimed, looking to see if Vera was paying him any attention. Thankfully, she wasn't, being busy orchestrating a smooth transition into dessert from a quick clean up.

"Aunt Edna, can I drive your Mustang later?"

"Will, you're a college man now, and the proper word is may, not can. May I drive your Mustang later, is the proper English."

"May I?" Will said, grinning at his favorite aunt pouring herself another adult drink.

"As long as your Mom and Dad say it's fine. Ask them after dessert."

"Cool. I will. Thanks, Aunt Edna."

"Aunt Edna, Rose and I have often wondered about your life. May we ask you a few questions?" The twins had always been interested in their aunt, and now they felt comfortable to ask more personal questions about her, seeing how they were college girls and more mature.

"Fire away, beautiful, while Willard and I enjoy another shot of bourbon," Edna answered, filling two glasses with three fingers of Edna's hard liquor of choice.

"Aunt Edna, are you rich?"

"What kind of question is that? Of course, I'm rich."

"Do you have tons of money?"

"No, I don't. Dear, there are plenty of people in this world who are poor with tons of money. Money does not make you rich."

"What does?"

"Willard, would you like to help me with this one?" Edna responded, tipping her glass towards her new drinking friend.

"Sure, I used to be rich with money," said Willard, "but I was poor like your Aunt said. Looking back, I can honestly say we were the wealthiest when we were the poorest," he responded, staring deeply into his glass of bourbon as a lonely tear rolled down his left cheek.

Edna saw the tear, sensing Willard's regrets were greater than she had imagined due to his current status in life. "Honey, I'm rich with all of the right things. Look around you here. There's wealth in each smiling face. I have my health, liquor, cigarettes, food, warmth, clothes, transportation, a huge house over my head, plenty of loved ones in my life, and I sleep like the dead. Yes, I'm rich."

"Have you been married?" fidgeting with a curl of her hair, Rose stated, shifting her weight forward to the edge if her chair towards her Aunt Edna.

"Nope. I never met a guy who could last longer than a fresh fifth of bourbon."

"What do you mean by your answer?" Will joined in, enjoying Edna's interesting and humorous descriptive answers.

"Oh, I've tasted a number of men over the years, but men are like this fifth of liquor. Sooner or later the bottle is empty, and I've enjoyed all they have to offer. If I could find one who'd fill my glass every time I wanted it, I'd probably marry the stiff."

"Edna, has your heart ever been destroyed?" Willard stated, shocking Edna with such an inquiry of seriousness from him. She had opted to maintain a sense of humor in answering her nieces and nephew. Initially, she thought there was no chance for a clever or humor-laced response to the worn man's question, but she was a master at wordplay, coming up with one.

"Willard, yes, I have. Last year, I wrecked my Mustang and had to go without it for a solid month. The Ford is like a twin sister. How about you, Willard?" Edna stated, lighting another thin cigarette.

"I've shattered three and completely crushed one," cryptically, Willard answered, lowering his head to conceal his trembling lips and tear-filled eyes.

Entering the room, carrying a pot of fresh coffee, Vera announced, "Dessert is ready. Dig in folks."

Willard's story would have to wait... for the moment.

136

Edna watched as tears rolled down the once rich, poor man's cheeks, dropping onto his sunken chest and Quincy's dress shirt.

Small talk accompanied dessert.

Silently, Willard sat while they ate, sipping alternately from a cup of black coffee and crystal glass of bourbon. Dessert was the farthest thing from his pensive mind.

"Vera, Willard and I were answering a few questions from the kids while you worked on dessert. They wanted to know about being rich, marriage, broken hearts, and other things. We were asked if our hearts had been broken. We answered. I explained my answer. Willard may have been about to explain his when y'all entered the dining room. Willard, do you wish to expand on your last answer. I know I'm curious as to what you meant."

All were seated at the table with eyes focused on their somber male guest, eating had ceased for the time being.

An eerie and nervous silence fell on the room before Willard finally spoke. "Like I said, I was rich once. We were wealthy and yet, so poor. My wife, two daughters, and I lived in the affluent Buckhead area of Atlanta. I was an engineer, graduating with a PhD in it from Georgia Tech. I designed a good number of the buildings in downtown Atlanta and up the Peachtree Road corridor. Despite all of my successes, I squandered what was pure and good in my life, climbing into a bottle and never crawling out. I hadn't realized my family was the only thing in my life worth having. The alcohol was a cold and cruel beast. Like each Thanksgiving, two days ago, I walked from Atlanta to Snellville to be with my family. At Walmart,

Quincy, you'd asked me if I had family in Snellville. I pointed to where they are. The three of them are buried in one grave in front of the church across from the store. My wife was from here. The one I pointed towards was her family's church," he explained, pausing briefly to wipe the tears from his face. Reaching over to him, Edna clutched his shaking left hand.

His story continued, "I put them there. I killed my family as surely as I'm sitting here. Booze comes with wealth. It's as much a status symbol as the Mercedes you drive or the mansion you own two doors down from the Governor of Georgia's home. My girls begged me to stop hurting mommy, to put an end to my drinking. My wife did everything in her power to support me emotionally, professionally, and spiritually. She pleaded with me to seek help. I didn't and wouldn't. I was in control of my own rotting empire. On Christmas Eve 2000, we had attended several parties during the day and evening. At the final one, our children were with us because Santa was making an appearance for all the rich kids. It was held at our country club. The finest alcohol was flowing. At my insistence, we had left the party early because I was angry with my wife and our crying girls. My wife begged me to allow her to drive us home, but it was my new Lexus. Verbally, we fought about it in front of the children. These fights had grown frequent. It was a bitterly cold night. Rain mixed with ice pounded the city. The streets were slick, and I continued drinking, guzzling from the fifth of Vodka I'd taken from the club. Speeding along winding roads in Buckhead is a certain recipe for disaster, being intoxicated doing so can be deadly. The police report said I left the roadway airborne, doing over ninety miles

139

per hour, smashing into a huge oak tree. On impact, my drunken body was thrown from the car. My daughters and wife burned to death as I lay in a cold ditch, listening to their screams. One by one, their suffering ended. My youngest daughter was the last to perish. To this day, I still hear their screams, pleading for their mother, me, and God to make it stop, to save them. I didn't have one scratch on me, not a single one. Edna, yes, I've shattered three hearts, destroying them forever, and irreparably. I've mutilated one."

Willard apologized to the family, thanking them for their kindness and generosity. He stood and walked towards the kitchen door, exiting the house.

Edna followed him.

Chapter 12. Mysterious Ways

While Edna and Willard were outside, the rest of the family and Lisa sat around the dinner table in stunned silence. There wasn't a dry eye among the group.

Wiping the moisture from his eyes, Quincy broke the silence. "There's no doubt in my mind God had a hand in this. Vera will tell you she had written 'two packages of rolls' on my grocery list. They weren't on it. She saw this. Y'all know Will and I were dispatched to Walmart to find rolls. This is where we encountered Willard. Aunt Edna is out there with him. She has a beautiful heart and pure soul. I'm certain His mysterious ways continue to unfold. Let's wipe these tears away and feel good about what we're witnessing. I don't know what will happen with Willard, but I do have faith in the Almighty and in the goodness of this family. Aunt Edna has a major role to play in all of this. I can feel it. Vera, this has been our best Thanksgiving ever. Thank each of you for making it so."

"Okay, enough tears. Ladies, let's make short work of this clean up. Quincy, you and the men head to the den. Kids, Lisa, we've got this. Isn't there a football game playing?" Vera stated, filling her hands with dessert dishes.

Entering the conversation, Ricki helped break the dire mood. "Mom, you have to tell us your secret spices you used on the turkey this year. It was the best turkey I've had."

Mom was not about to spill the real recipe.

Quincy wasn't as protective, launching into the frozen turkey debacle, tumbling in the dryer with lilac seasoning.

The kids, Lisa, and husbands weren't about to miss this reveal. No one opted to rest, helping with the table clearing, cleaning, and dish washing.

Outside, Edna and Willard were deep in conversation.

"Willard, where do you live?" Edna inquired, holding both of his hands.

"Sixteen years ago, I walked away from my house, business, and money, losing it all. I'll sleep at Atlanta missions or the Salvation Army a day or two each week. Mostly, I sleep beneath the stars."

"How do you afford to eat?"

"I don't really. People will give me a few coins or a buck or two, thinking I'll use the money to feed myself. But I drink it away. When I have to eat, I'll either sober up a day and wait in the soup kitchen line near the mission, or, most of the time, I'll eat from the trash cans in and downtown Atlanta. You'd be shocked at the food people waste."

"How about your belongings, clothing and such?"

"I keep the little I have in a shopping bag. I left it under the tree at Walmart. It'll be there when I walk back."

"Willard, you're an intelligent, handsome, and caring man. I'd love to help you, if you'll accept it. I could use a friend, a man, a companion in my life. I'll never ask you to do anything in return. You're welcome to live with me. I'll take care of you, and you'll look after me."

"Edna, that's too kind of you, but I'm no good. I'm broken."

"Don't say such about yourself. You've been going through a horrible sequence of nightmares. Maybe, it's time to bury the past, to begin to forgive yourself, and live again. God has forgiven you. I know this. I have a spacious home in Buckhead and enough money for us. You can move back to north Atlanta with me. We'll have many adventures together, if you want. I'm lonely, and frankly, I could use the company and conversations. We'd be helping each other."

"Edna, today felt good. It was like I was alive again, a feeling I haven't experienced for many years. I think you're right. It's time to reclaim my life or at least, try to recapture the good parts of life. If I agree to do this, what will your family say? They won't appreciate seeing you help an old drunk like me."

"Bull crap, Willard Jones! My family will embrace the idea and you. Just say yes and you'll see how great those folks inside this home are."

"Okay, I'm in. Let's do it," Willard agreed, feeling a pleasant excitement building within himself.

"Let's tell the family. Allow me to handle it. They're used to this eccentric relative doing insane stuff."

They entered the kitchen.

"Vera, Quincy, gang, Willard's coming home with me to Buckhead. He's going to live with me. Kids, I think I've found a perfect drink."

The announcement could not have been better received.

"Edna, I've made you two plates of food to bring home with you... with desserts. They're in the fridge," Vera announced, knowing in advance something marvelous was brewing outside.

"Willard, let's see if we can find more clothing for you. Vera's been after me for a year to go through my closet. I think this 'in a minute' can be accomplished in a hurry," Quincy said, leading Willard for the second time towards the couple's bedroom.

Cindy proclaimed the day to be a huge success. "Mom, consider this, there hasn't been one fire engine, ambulance, or police unit called to this house this Thanksgiving."

"Cindy, you're right, and my new kitchen is still intact," Vera responded. Laughter filled the brick ranch once again.

Chapter 13. Going Home

Glenda and Lisa were the first couple to say thank you and goodbye.

Edna and Willard were next to depart.

Walking to her Mustang, Willard stated, "Edna, would it be alright by you if we stopped by the cemetery? I want to say goodbye to my girls."

"Certainly, we can." She drove him the three short miles to the church and cemetery, leaving him alone while he spoke to his family.

Back at the Johns' home, Cindy and her family were the last to leave.

Cuddling on their couch, Vera and Quincy sat quietly, staring at a silent television.

Edna and Willard drove westbound towards Atlanta... going home.

Excerpt from Ron Shaw's novelette:

The Rebooted

1. Opportunity Knocks

At dusk, three loud knocks at her front door scared the young, grief-stricken mother of four. Huddling around her in front of a solitary space heater, Ann's three children jumped, startling her even more. For a brief second, they shivered, fearing it was death itself that had come knocking.

It was Halloween evening, but at 1010 Peyton Avenue, there was no cause for celebration. As usual, there was no candy waiting to be dispensed to the neighborhood goblins, hobos, princesses, and ghouls, looking for sugary treats. Her children would miss this trick or treat.

Mrs. Ann May could barely fill the stomachs living under the leaking roof of her dilapidated, two-room rental.

This late October there was one less child for her to feed.

A week earlier, her youngest son, Russell had been struck by a soda delivery truck less than a block away from their small house. The boy lay in a coma on life support at Atlanta Memorial Hospital. If the treating neurologist's prognosis was correct, the little boy's life would soon end at the age of eight.

After the accident, staying by his side for the first four days and nights, his mother prayed as never before, begging God, someone, anyone to help her

146

son. The doctors offered no chance of recovery. The machines were all that stood between Russell and death.

In a surreal mixture of profound grief, agony, and disbelief she anguished, dreading the decision that was ultimately hers alone to make. Compounding the impoverished family's dire situation, there was no father present, no step dad, no insurance policy, and zero money.

Frightened, the four stared at each other, momentarily frozen, hoping bad news would go away.

"You kids be quiet. Don't answer the door," Ann whispered.

Two fresh, louder, and quicker knocks answered her whispers. Wayne, the oldest, stood. Walking to the door, he softly stated, "Mom, we have to. It might be about Russell. Maybe, it's good news." Opening the flimsy door, Wayne glumly, greeted the two, well-dressed men, standing with hats in hand, "Yes, sirs, can we help you?"

The taller of the two answered, "Son, we're here to speak with a Mrs. Ann May. I assume she is your mother, and if so, that would make you Wayne. Am I correct?

"Yes sir, you are. Mom, these men want to talk with you." Reluctantly, Ann walked to the door, staring at the floor the entire time. With head down she said, "What can I do for you?"

"Mrs. May, I'm Joseph Thomas, and this is my business partner, Fred Wilson. Under the tragic circumstances, it's still our pleasure to meet you. Please, accept our deepest sympathy about your son and for what your entire family is going through. We're doctors, and we're certain that we can help your son, you, and your family."

"What do you mean? We don't have any money to buy anything you're selling." Shyly, Ann responded without making eye contact.

Mr. Wilson replied, "It's chilly out this evening. May we come inside and discuss our proposal? We assure you that we're not trying to sell you anything. What we have to offer will cost you nothing, and in fact, we may be able to assist you financially."

"Come on in, then. Travis, go bring two chairs from the kitchen for these men."

With satchel and what appeared to be a typewriter case also in hand, the men in business suits entered, taking their seats.

With his brief case laying across his lap, Doctor Thomas continued, "Mrs. May, I'll attempt to explain everything straightforwardly and as simply as possible.

"We deeply regret the circumstances surrounding this visit, yet, we are excited and optimistic at the prospect of bringing Russell home to you, well and whole again.

"We were contacted for a patient consultation by Atlanta Memorial Hospital officials where your son is being treated. Treating physicians from this State of Georgia experimental hospital will do this when they have a patient whom they believe could be helped by our company. We've completed our preliminary medical assessment. Russell is an excellent patient for of our treatment.

"I apologize. I'm getting a bit ahead of myself. Doctor Wilson and I represent a USA medical, technological, and neurological research and development company named MWS. It is a subsidiary of a larger, global corporation, The Lazarus Collective.

"I, Doctor Wilson, and our staff will personally implement, monitor, and oversee all aspects of our treatment regiment for your boy. There are no medications used, no injections given, and no invasive medical procedures conducted, whatsoever. Our entire involvement in treating your son will take six days or a total of one hundred and forty-four hours."

Her children listened intently to every word. Their mother was lost in a murky, mental maze, smoking her cigarette, eyes fixated on the lapping flames of the space heater. She was overwhelmed.

Breaking the awkward silence, Wayne inquired, "Mom, did you hear what the man said?"

"Son, be quiet now. Let the grown-ups speak.

"I heard him say a lot. I've listened to way too much talk from doctors this week.

"How are you going to help Russell? Tell me what you can do to save his life or at least, free him from those damnable machines. He's in the good Lord's hands now."

At this statement, papers were removed from Doctor Thomas's briefcase, and Doctor Wilson gingerly retrieved a small device of some kind from his carrying case. The room was dimly lit, adding to the tension, fear, and mystery for the Mays.

"Mrs. May, like I've said, our treatment for your son will take only six days. If you sign the release and waiver forms I have here for us to go forward, we'll begin early tomorrow morning.

"Our involvement with this medical case is pre-approved and completely sanctioned by the hospital, but you'll also be required to sign a waiver of responsibility for the attending physicians, nurses, and hospital. The signed release forms for treatment and waiver are mandatory for us to continue.

"My colleague, Doctor Wilson, will explain the six-day process and equipment to you. Doctor Wilson."

"Yes. While the two pieces of equipment we will use for Russell may appear ordinary or somewhat simple. They are not. It has taken decades and hundreds of millions of dollars to invent these devices, improving them from model to model to their present state. The other things we'll use are our portable, interfaced, computer device and our main, central computer at MWS. The small device I use wirelessly connects everything. It is no larger than an iPad Mini, but it's memory capabilities are extraordinary. Everything I carry and use are digital. There are no unsightly wires, bulky switches, or other such cumbersome machinery.

"The cap, that's what we call it, fits over the head of the patient not unlike in appearance and comfort that of a stocking or skull cap. It will not cover the eyes of the patient. Its interior is lined with dozens of tiny sensors that monitor brain activity, receive, and record the slightest signals of neurological life. But as you can see, as I turn the cap inside out, they are unexposed. It also transmits stimuli programming as well as monitoring brain function, and recording experiences within the brain, such as dreams.

"I apologize for how dry and boring this technology lingo may sound.

"The patient's visor monitor with head strap is used primarily with subjects who are conscious. But whether eyes are closed or open, the patient or wearer will see our program feeds whether from our library or from the patient's mental, event recordings. Mrs. May, while Russell is in a coma, we will not have to use the visor. If and when he regains consciousness, we may use it if he is still under treated during the six-day program.

"If you wish, in a minute or two, I'll allow you and your children to see what these items can do. A brief session under the cap is worth more than a ton of verbal descriptions and explanations.

"If we are able to begin in the morning with Russell, we will spend the first twenty-four hours monitoring your son's entire brain. It's a scientific fact that the overwhelming majority of people use a mere ten percent or less of their brain's capacity. That means there is at least ninety or more percent of our brain sits dormant. If we are able to tap into this massive, dormant area of the brain, the possibilities may be endless.

"I assure you that at this moment your son has activity going on in various parts of his injured brain.

"Our cap will document this activity, the locations of life, and hopefully, provide us with a better diagnosis and prognosis for Russell. We have seen patients come out of their comas during the first phase of our program. Others have done so before the three phases were completed. A number of them have done so days after the process. We are very proud of our success rate, but there is always room for improvement

"During the second phase, we'll run non-stop, visually stimulating, education oriented, and targeted programming for forty-eight hours for a child of your son's age. Russell's brain will be challenged to react, flooding it with stimuli like never before.

"In some ways, the final phase is the most critical. Within the first twenty-four hours of this phase, we'll repeat monitoring his brain's activity, recording any dreams he may be having. This phase's second twenty-four hour period will be filled with more stimuli. The final day will consist of recording only what is happening inside your son's brain.

"Within a day or two, after the program, we will be able to show you what your son has experienced within his brain. By this time, we strongly believe Russell will be close to coming home whole and well again.

"Before I demonstrate the devices, do you have any questions, Mrs. May?"

"No. Let Wayne, the oldest, try it. He'll tell us what it's like." The other children weren't disappointed with this decision. They had come to see their older brother as a figurative father in their lives. They trusted him implicitly. Reluctantly, he assumed the position with visions of vacating the unfair burden as soon as possible.

Placing the cap and visor on Wayne, Mr. Wilson stated, "Son, do you like baseball?"

"Yes sir, I do," shot from the mouth of the boy who had thirteen demanding years behind him.

The doctor keyed in a program from his small device, playing it for the teen.

Instantly, sitting erect in his chair, Wayne's mouth gapped open. Mr. Wilson and Thomas smiled as the boy took in his first World Series game, perching on the edge of his seat behind Home plate at Yankee Stadium. They knew what he was experiencing and what he'd eventually watch as Babe Ruth hit the series-winning home run. Running the bases alongside the Babe would be Wayne May.

A brief time later, the program was concluded. The thirteen-year-old sat there speechless for a minute or two before exploding with excitement, describing what he'd experienced.

"Mom, I was there at Yankee Stadium. I saw the Babe win the series. He shook my hand and gave me an autographed ball, signing on the sweet spot, too. I ran the bases with him. I could hear, taste, feel, and see everything going on around me. It was as real as me looking at y'all. I could smell the hot dogs, beer, and freshly-cut grass on the field. I ate roasted peanuts and had a cold root beer. Sitting beside me, a large man was smoking a big cigar. It stunk awful, and a slight breeze would blow his smoke into my face every now and again.

"Then, after the game, while the fans were still going crazy with the players huddled and celebrating on the field, I became an Eagle, flying over the entire stadium, watching everything. I circled the stadium a few times and after that, I flew over New York City. It wasn't scary or anything, but I could fly.

"Holy hell... wow!"

"Son, stop cussing.

"Mr. Thomas, Mr. Wilson, if there's a chance to save my son, I can't turn it down. I'll sign your papers. Please, bring my boy back home, back from death."

"Mrs. May, we'll do the best we can for Russell. If things do not occur as we anticipate, seeing that you're of meager financial means, for participating in this program, our company will assist you financially with any arrangement costs you might incur."

"Mr. Thomas, just bring my boy home, alive and well. We don't need your financial help. You're already giving us enough. Hope is plenty."

"Thank you, Mrs. May.

"We would request that the you and your children refrain from visiting your son over the next six days. We will keep you abreast of his condition as the treatment proceeds. I know this sounds harsh, but we and Russell will need every minute to possibly save his life over the next one hundred and forty-four hours. Be assured that if there is any news, positive or not, we will contact you in person or by phone. Do you have a phone?"

"We don't have a phone, but our next door neighbor, Mrs. Watts, has offered to allow us use her phone for incoming and outgoing calls. I put her number on your forms. She said no matter the time we could use her phone. To receive calls for us is also fine. She's a kind lady."

Gathering their signed paperwork and securing their equipment, the two men left the grieving family, assuring Ann and her children they would do their best for Russell, beginning the following morning.

To continue reading *The Rebooted* by Ron Shaw, please go here: (Amazon) or here:(Barnes and Noble)

Excerpt from Ron Shaw's Novelette:

Uya: A Beast Like No Other

1. The Payne Farm

The unusual livestock killings began in earnest the first frost of 2016. Such was the way of life and death for the rural farming community of the North Georgia mountains, but near the Georgia and Tennessee border, the farmers had experienced nothing like the gluttony of carnage to come. It would become a feasting.

Chickens seemed to be the favored meal of "Uya"... especially the bird's blood. When it had started in Georgia, a few smaller farm animals also fell prey to the ravenous creature, walking on all fours, dragging a strange, hairless-bodied, and pointed tail behind it. Thus far, Uya's description was based solely on tracks.

The next Georgia victims of its blood feast were Tom Payne's thirteen chickens, consisting of twelve "layers" and his prized Rhode Island Red rooster. Each bird had first been drained of blood before the meat and most of the bones were devoured.

Tom and his wife, Jill owned a small farm not ten miles from Dahlonega, Georgia. They had lived here for close to six years after moving from Atlanta in search of a less cluttered life. Their nearest neighbor was five miles away which meant no one other than he and his wife would suffer from the frequent crying of a newborn daughter suffering from colic.

Until being informed by a county deputy sheriff who responded to the Payne's 911 call, Tom didn't know the critter had previously been named by a Tennessee farmer and volunteer fireman. He is one-half Native American — a Cherokee. Several times he'd assisted local law agencies in trying to track and hopefully, destroy the beast. His most recent hunt came after Uya ravaged several calves of a neighbor. He was an excellent tracker. He'd named the evil spirit Uya who to the Cherokee was an evil earth spirit which is invariably opposed to the forces of right and light. He'd also referred to it as "Night Beast."

Responding to the Payne call was the North Georgia, Lumpkin County, K-9 handler, Deputy Lane. Tom and Jill Payne were advised of the culprit's ravenous exploits from just over the line into Tennessee and a few more incidents in Georgia attributed to the supposed animal.

Before the day was over, the deputy and Tom would attempt to track Uya.

"Deputy, what kind of animal do you think did this?"

"Mr. Payne, I don't know. Nobody has a good idea about that. A few say it could be an extremely large raccoon or maybe a wild dog. Based on the few poor tracks I've seen and heard about from others who've hunted the killer, I'd include a wolf, boar, or large coyote to their list, but my gut and this old bloodhound's telling me different."

"What do you mean by that?"

"For one thing, last night, when the feeding was happening, did you hear any unusual noises from your chicken coop?"

"We didn't."

"Mr. Payne, don't you find that odd since a baker's dozen were taken?"

"You're right. That's strange."

"Also, based on our past cases similar to yours and even before we begin tracking, I'd guess each bird was taken one at a time, carried a short distance outside the coop and feasted upon."

"That sounds right based on the one I found."

"Did anything out of the ordinary happen last night during the morning hours?"

"Not really. Betsy, our newborn, has a case of colic, and she woke me at around three AM, crying. Deciding to let Jill sleep, I went to her. Walking her around the house and rocking her a bit usually calms her. I did this for about half an hour. When she was sleeping again, I placed her back in her crib and headed to our bed. I can see the chicken coop from her window. If anything was wrong there, I'd have heard or seen it."

"What time did you discover there was a problem?"

"I woke at six before sunrise, and like normal, started the coffee, and then, I went out to feed the animals. The livestock was fed first. They're in the barn and directly behind it on the other side of the house. After that, I discovered the hole in the fence where the critter had entered the coop yard. Other than a few extra stray feathers laying about and the missing birds, there was nothing else of note to see inside the fence and coop. No blood. No nothing."

"Yep, this fiend is clever... more so than any of the animals on the culprit list. With one bite, it breaks the chicken's neck, killing it silently without a sound from the victim."

"Oh, there was one weird thing I noticed while inside the hen house. It was the most awful stench I've smelled. It was gagging putrid."

"Yep. I was meaning to ask you about that. This thing's smart and foul-smelling."

"Deputy, could it be a bear? I know they're crafty like raccoons."

"The reason a bear didn't make the list of possible culprits is based on the attacker's bizarre tracks. No one can explain them. They aren't bear tracks. I'm not the only one who's hit the internet, Googling for possible answers. Don't tell anyone I told you, but if we do find prints indicating it walks upright on two legs, La Chupacabra would be at the top of my creature lineup."

"Deputy, is there anything else peculiar about this animal?"

"If my hunch is right, when we find the rest of the remains, you'll see more weird traits for a carnivore. By the way, where'd you locate the first remains?"

"They were just to the east of the coop at the tree line. It was as if it used the first tree to hide behind while ripping the rooster apart. That's odd. The rooster was chosen and eaten first."

"Mr. Payne, that tells me it's smarter than I even thought, taking out the worst threat first."

"Deputy, tell me more about the weird traits."

"Sure. Even its teeth marks we've found on collected bones are peculiar. This one likes to have his drink before his meal and always in that order. It'll drain the blood from the jugular before eating whatever is wanted, including bones on some but not all. It also has a taste for marrow. Let's see if we can track him. Mr. Payne, if you would, always stay slightly behind and to the left or right of me and my dog, keeping your shotgun barrel pointed away from me and my dog. Point it towards the ground. We don't want any accidents in the woods," the deputy instructed.

"Will do, officer."

Following the direction of the carnage, the armed men and bloodhound searched the woods for about three hours, finding eleven of the remaining carcasses of the other birds. One wasn't located. After losing the scent in a large swampy area, their search ended.

The deputy had retrieved a few batches of hair, blood, bones, and feathers from the hunt. Like at the coop, digital pictures were also taken in the woods of the scenes, remains, and sparse tracks left by the predator.

After returning to the farm, an official incident report was made, and a case number was given to Mr. Payne.

"Sir, ma'am, call me if there's anything further you can think of about this case and especially in a hurry, if any other attacks happen. Oh, if you get the chance, use that 12 gauge with double-aught buckshot on it. I'd like nothing better to come out and retrieve its body, whatever Uya is. Be careful."

"We will. Thank you, Deputy Lane."

"Sure thing. I'll be in touch with you if I have anything new to report. Here's my card with my phone numbers on it. Call me any time, day or night."

"Good afternoon, officer," Jill added.

"Goodday, Mrs. Payne, Mr. Payne."

To continue reading, *Uya, a Beast Like No Other*, please order here:

http://amzn.to/2v9KLNv

About the Author-Ron Shaw

Ron Shaw is an Atlanta, Georgia, native who currently resides in Gwinnett County, Georgia, with his wife and daughter. He attended Roosevelt High School in Atlanta and continued his education at Mercer University in Macon, Georgia for two years. Ron met his future wife in Atlanta after his second year at Mercer and transferred his junior year to Georgia State University.

In 1973, with new responsibilities, he became an Atlanta Police Officer while attending college full time. Ron attained a BA degree in English Literature from Georgia State University in 1974. He retired from the Atlanta Police Department in 1996 after a very fulfilling and personally satisfying career.

Ron is an award-winning cover designer, best-selling, and prolific author, writing in a wide variety of genres. His novels are; Seven Fish Tree, The Yellow Bus Boys, Transmutation: The Life of a twisted Cop, RED, The Yellow Bus Boys Go Blue Canada Bound. He co-authored a novel with Texas author, D.A. Grady entitled Around The Campfire: Two Badge Toters' Tales. Ron has three novellas and a short story in his paranormal/historical romance Cramped Quarters series, consisting of Mary's Trunk, Mary's Journey Begins, Mary's Journey Continues, and Paul's Story.

His published short story, The Dead and the Dying, also appears in the horror anthology, Dark Tales. Another of Ron's published short stories, J, also appears in the anthology, Short & Fun Stories, Vol. 1.

To showcase his brother-in-law's photography, Ron recently published, Photography by J. Robert Sosby.

His adult novel, RED has been translated into French.

He and poet Richard M. Knittle, Jr. have published a collaboration of poetry and photography entitled Poetry East To West. It contains photographs by J. Robert Sosby and Richard M. Knittle, Jr., accentuating the poems by Richard and Ron.

He has four books of poetry, containing superb photography (courtesy of his brother-in-law, J. Robert Sosby and poet, Richard M. Knittle, Jr.), Without From Within: Poems by Ron Shaw (available in English and French), TraVerses: Poems by Ron Shaw, Southern Brewed Poetry, and Poetry East To West.

His latest works are novelettes, Christmas Past: An Angel's Story, The Rebooted, Uya: A Beast Like No Other, a boxed set, Novelettes and Short Stories. Recently, Ron has re-edited and republished his first two novels with new covers, Seven Fish Tree and The Yellow Bus Boys. He plans to do the same in 2017 with his third novel, Transmutation: The Life of a Twisted Cop.

He can be easily contacted through his website at ronshawmedia.com, Twitter at @RonGizmo, Facebook at Author Ron Shaw, and at Google+ as Ron Shaw.

Also by Ron Shaw

Seven Fish Tree

The Yellow Bus Boys

Transmutation: The Life of a Twisted Cop

Mary's Trunk (Cramped Quarters Book 1)

Mary's Journey Begins (Cramped Quarters Book 2)

Mary's Journey Continues (Cramped Quarters Book 3)

Paul's Story (Cramped Quarters Book 4)

RED

Dark Tales

The Dead and the Dying

Around The Campfire: Two Badge-Toters' Tales

J (a short story within the anthology, Fun & Short Stories)

The Yellow Bus Boys Go Blue: Canada Bound

Without From Within: Poems by Ron Shaw

Dans L'Abime Interieur: Poemes par Ron Shaw

Dans L'Abime Interieur Recueil Deux: Poemes par Ron Shaw

Without From Within: Dans L'Abime Interieur Recueils Un & Deux

Dans L'Abime Interieur Recueils Un & Deux: Without From Within

TraVerses: Poems by Ron Shaw

Christmas Past: An Angel's Story

Southern Brewed Poetry

The Rebooted

Photography by J. Robert Sosby

RED (French edition)

Novelettes and Short Stories

Short & Fun Stories

Poetry East To West

Uya: A Beast Like No Other

The Witness
Dorothy May Mercer

The Witness

Wednesday, April 26, 2017, 4:30 AM

Two days ago, I witnessed an accident during which a man died. Since then, sleeping is difficult.

Dave and I were heading over to Mt. Pleasant, from our home in Canadian Lakes. We were happy and running ahead of schedule. It was a little after three, and we had plenty of time to get to our destination, the Soaring Eagle Hotel. Check-in wasn't until four.

Unlike my usual habit, I was ready early, packed and eager to go almost an hour ahead of time. Dave was ready, too, and so we decided we might as well leave. If our room wasn't ready yet, we could just look around the amazing hotel.

Nevertheless, something happened to delay us for a few minutes. Was it a devine destiny or a mere phone call? I do not remember. But something happened that caused us to be delayed just exactly long enough to be at that place at that particular time--in time to be witnesses. A few seconds either way would have saved us the sad encounter.

It was a gorgeous spring day, sunny, clear and dry. The grass was just showing its first promising carpet of emerald green and the leaves were that soft leafy-

163

green color they are when they first start coming out. It had been a long winter. We were hoping to see spring daffodils and tulips on the hotel grounds.

Our car had just left the stop sign where we turned the corner at the retirement home from Buchanan onto 90th avenue, now headed north Were there other cars approaching from the oncoming lanes? Possibly. Dave was driving and so I was gazing out the window, paying no attention to traffic. There was little traffic on the two-lane country highway. In fact I was blissfully unaware of any other cars around us, either behind or oncoming. We were not all alone on the road, but I took no notice.

Dave was not going very fast, just moseying along, happy to be heading toward a free overnight at the hotel. Dave had received it as a gift since he is a veteran and it was his birthday month. The hotel does that for vets.

Suddenly I spied something strange on the grass ahead of us on the opposite side of the road. In that instant it looked at first like some sort of whirlwind. It was something spinning on the grass, spinning so fast that it appeared as a blur. I asked, "What's that?" In retrospect, I believe that Dave and I saw it in the same instant. In the next moment I exclaimed, "Dave, it's a motorcycle!" Dave slowed the car and stopped off the road opposite the motorcycle, which was now lying on the grass, in the shallow ditch or indentation which is normally constructed alongside any road.

"Oh my gosh, there's a man!" I exclaimed, immediately reaching for my brand new cell phone, as Dave leaped from the car and ran across to the man. The man was lying on his back beside the motorcycle, on the side away from my line of sight. His body was partially obscured to my vision by the motorcycle which was now lying on its side. I could see his legs and the lower half of his body. Another woman was there with Dave and they stood over the man while I frantically tried to call 911.

To my recollection, Dave called to me, "Call 911." I was trying, but I couldn't make my phone come on. And so, I grabbed Dave's new phone and pushed the "on" button. His phone is different, but I knew enough to tap the phone icon. Another screen came up that I did not recognize. I tapped the phone button more times, but did not know (at that time) what to do next, to make it work. It was one of those occasions that people describe when time stood still, but it could not have been more than a few seconds. Realizing I did not know how to do this, I left the car and called to Dave, "I can't make it work."

"It's okay, we've got it," he said as I dashed across the road to meet him and hand him the phone.

Dave had been merely standing there observing the lady as she was apparently on the phone talking to someone. The man's body was still partially obscured to me by the motorcycle. I could see her bending over him, but I could not see her touch him.

A motorcycle helmet lay on the grass a few feet away from the machine, apparently having flown off before the machine skidded to the ground. I suggested to Dave. "Why don't you take some pictures?" I knew that the authorities might need them. And so Dave snapped a few shots with his cell phone's camera function.

Shortly another car stopped and a strong-looking man ran up and started doing CPR immediately. I stood back across the road, to stay out of the way. A white van stopped off the road ahead of me from which a

165

man emerged to stand beside me. I said to him, "Someone should call 911."

He started calling and was soon talking to them and telling them where we were, saying "A man is down."

Another man ran up and took turns with the person doing CPR.

As the CPR silently continued, we all held our breath for what seemed like an interminable time before the siren sounded in the distance. But it was actually only a few minutes. Finally a welcome sight–a State Police car arrived. An officer leaped out, grabbed some kind of kit from his trunk and opened it on the ground. He ran up to the body and started doing something.

A few cars had slowed and continued carefully by the scene. Thinking that we did not want another accident, I suggested to the man from the white van that someone should direct traffic. And so he moved up ahead of us and started doing just that.

Two men wearing matching T shirts that identified them as some kind of volunteer group had run up and started assisting the State policeman.

In time another State Police car arrived, partially cutting off the traffic lane across from me. Thus the traffic was slowed down to one lane at a time. Dave had started helping the man coordinate the cars through, one at a time. The man suggested Dave move down and catch the cars coming in the other lane, and so together he and Dave directed cars to slow and move by, one at a time.

Finally an EMT van arrived. Two men ran to the scene where they applied a machine that took over the CPR.

Dave was no longer needed to direct traffic and so he joined me beside the road. We watched for a while and then decided that we should get out of the way. Dave walked over to speak to an officer, telling him we were leaving and giving him our names. I found my business card in my purse and walked over to give it to the officer. He took our names and verified our address. He thanked me. Dave gave him a brief account of what we saw.

After thanking the officer for "being there" we got into our car and slowly moved forward as a sheriff's car pulled up from the north. As we neared the next corner to turn right opposite the County Park, another EMT vehicle rounded that corner. Dave motioned out the window, pointing the way ahead. We turned the corner toward Mt. Pleasant and continued on.

After a lovely stay at the hotel, we returned home the next day. Dave looked up online and found an article saying that the man had been pronounced dead at the scene. He was from Big Rapids, only fifty years old.

Dave and I speculated on what caused the accident. In and of itself, we could see no cause. Actually the crash did not appear to be that serious. The cycle just went off the road, spun and slid down on the grass. The man was not thrown through the air. He was lying on the grass, on his back right next to the motorcycle. He must have slid off after it stopped, or as it was stopping.

We did not see him go off the road, and were not aware of any other vehicle involved. We wondered whether the cycle blew a tire, but, at first glance, it did not seem to have any damage. We wondered whether the driver may have had some physical problem that caused him to lose control.

Assuming the authorities would figure out what happened, we wondered would they call us for a statement? Yes, indeed, a female officer called us after supper the next day, Tuesday evening.

Would we ever hear from anyone again? Most likely not. It was all over for us and we were on our way in about half an hour. We witnessed a man die. How very sad.

An hour ago I awoke out of a sound sleep, remembering this. I'm a writer. Maybe writing it down would allow me to sleep again.

It is now 5:34 AM.

Goodbye sweet man. Perhaps we will meet again, someday.

Update. Wednesday

I learned his name was Steven M-----.

When I read this story to Dave, he confirmed what I wrote, and added a few details of his own. He and the woman were the first ones to run up. She was some kind of health care professional and seemed to know how to take his vital signs. She reported that to someone on the phone. She and Dave asked the man questions such as "Can you hear me?" To which he merely moaned a couple times and did not move. His unblinking eyes were wide open. Dave heard her describing his condition as no heart beat or pulse, and shallow breathing. In a few moments she asked Dave if he knew CPR. Dave answered yes, knowing it had been maybe fifty years since his training. As Dave moved toward the man to begin pressing on the man's chest, another younger man ran up at top speed,

168

jumped on the victim and began vigorously applying CPR immediately.

Dave remarked that the Lord saved him at that moment. "If I had done CPR," he said, "I would have lived forever with the regret of having lost the man."

As it turned out, Dave was awake in the middle of the night, same as I, reliving the event.

Think of the number of people involved, whom Steve's loved ones will never know. Will they always wonder what happened?

Imagine this: policemen and first responders go through this every day. They live with the memories every night. Dave and I only did once.

An Evening with a Candidate
Dorothy May Mercer

Let's face it—when one lives out in the boonies, unless it is in Iowa or New Hampshire—one does not expect to encounter many US presidential candidates. And so, when we learned that Senator Marco Rubio was holding a rally in Grand Rapids, Michigan, only seventy miles away, we immediately put in our bid for two tickets. It was the fall of 2016.

In short order the tickets appeared in my Inbox, suitable for printing.

There was a little confusion about the starting time. Email estimates ranged from 6:15 PM to 7:30 PM. But, as the day grew closer the time settled down to "6:30 PM the Doors Open, 7:30 to 8:15 Program."

Thus informed, David and I dined at 4:30 PM and left home in our automobile a quarter-hour later. Our target address was Lacks Enterprises, in the 4900 block of Broadmoor SE. "Can't imagine why they would pick Lacks Enterprises," Dave remarked.

"Never heard of it, have you?" I answered.

"Nope. Wonder what they do."

"Strange name," I observed. "Probably because it's handy to the airport." I counted off the numbers on the buildings as we drew near. "Ah, there is it...Lacks Enterprises."

Dave pulled into the right hand lane behind a short line of cars. It was nearly six o'clock and already people were lined up at the side door waiting to get in. "Oops, the driveway is barricaded," Dave noticed. As we drew closer I rolled down the window. A uniformed attendant spoke to us, "Take a right at the next light, and then a right on East Paris."

"Okay, thanks." I rolled up the window. Following his directions we passed building after building, with more gates and "Lacks" signs. The place went on and on. It was huge! Gigantic! Lacks Enterprises took up the whole quarter section, right in the middle of the industrial area of the City of Kentwood. We were being routed around to the back entrance. At last we came to an open gate, outlined with orange barricades and uniformed men with flashlights wearing bright orange vests, waving us in and onward to a parking spot on the grass berm. We grabbed our stuff and hurried to join the crowd standing at the back of a long line. It was disappointing to see that we were probably not going to get a front row seat.

We had worn our light-weight spring jackets, thinking it would be stifling hot inside the auditorium. Too bad for us, by six o'clock, the mild temperature of the day had dropped precipitously. An eight mile per hour breeze in our faces, added to the wind-chill factor. At the last minute, I had grabbed a blanket out of the back seat, but Dave had left his warm gloves in the car.

In no time the line of folks stretched out-of-sight behind us. We stomped our feet and huddled together, wrapped in our blanket, hoping the doors would open early. Didn't happen.

At last the line started moving. We filed past a graveyard of Links Enterprises semi-trucks, parking lots and more buildings. As we neared the yawning entrance we noted the clutch of television vans bordering the area. Finally we came within the shadow of the building, into its protection on the lee side, out of the wind. A half-dozen Rubio workers were lined up with scanners, checking tickets. In seconds the main computers would record my name, address, email address, phone number, party affiliation and exactly how much money I had donated to various charities and political causes.

Anxious to find seats we hurried by more tables displaying items for sale, Rubio-for-President buttons, placards and posters. Inside the vast warehouse, I realized to my dismay, there were no seats left. Already the crowd was standing six deep surrounding a makeshift stage, back-dropped in huge Rubio-for-President banners. I stretched to my full height, unable to see beyond the heads in front of me. Darn!

A helpful usher suggested we circle around to the other side of the crowd where we might find some chairs or at least a better view. We hurried onward, skirting behind the media platform and past the waiting patrons, to the far side. Alas, not only was the crowd six deep, but the tall men seemed to be in front. Well, there was nothing else to do but pick a spot and stake our claim.

No sooner had we settled-in than Dave announced he was leaving to use a bathroom...well...portable bathroom better known as a porta-potty. "Now, you will stay right here. Don't move, okay? I'll find you," he instructed.

"Okay," I nodded, putting on a brave front.

Little by little the crowd pressed closer. I worked to keep a space for Dave, using my elbows and leaning here and there. A nice gentleman behind me asked, "Excuse me, do you mind if I stand there?" as he pointed to the miniscule space beside me.

"Oh dear, please don't. I'm saving this space for my husband. He went to the Porta-potty."

Several folks nearby nodded in understanding and proceeded to help me keep a small space open.

For an interminable length of time, I watched in vain for Dave's arrival, as the depth of the crowd grew exponentially from six to twelve to eighteen, until I could no longer see the end of it. How would Dave find me, now, when everything had changed? While everyone else was facing forward in anticipation of the arrival of celebrities, I faced the back, standing on tiptoe, straining to spot Dave. I had almost given up when I spied his dear head moving along the edges. I waved and shouted, until he saw me and moved through the crowd to my place. "What a crowd!" he grumbled, "I had to wait in line!"

I nodded. "Now you know what it's like for women," I quipped.

With naught else to do, we waited, and waited and…

Nothing happened except for more tall men, clothed in black, moving into the front of the crowd lining up like a living fence, presumably to keep the fans from getting too close to the senator.

We expected there to be a rock band to entertain us as we waited. Not!

Well, at least, there should be a local politician or two to warm up the crowd-Not!

No band, no politicians--only a technician testing out the sound system, counting down from ten to five. From time to time amateur cheerleaders led the crowd in chanting, Mar-co, Ru-bio, Mar-co, Ru-bio, never lasting more than a couple of minutes before the echo petered out. I checked my watch. 7:15 PM. Only fifteen more minutes to go, that is, if the program started on time. Ruefully, I thought of President Obama's practice of always being late, sometimes a half hour or more.

Would Rubio be like Obama? Meanwhile I had taken up an exercise, in place, weaving from one foot to the other, with an added twist. I checked my watch, again. Only two minutes had passed.

"Want to leave?" Dave suggested in my ear. I shook my head. "No, not yet."

"It's an experience," he said. "Together."

"Yes, an experience," I nodded. "Together." I slid my arm around his waist and rocked some more.

We noticed a few supporters holding Rubio signs, taking the seats of honor on-stage, carefully arranged underneath the banners, for the TV cameras. I had dressed with a large red neck scarf and a Party lapel pin, foolishly hoping I would be chosen to sit behind the candidate. No such luck.

At 7:25 PM, someone took the microphone and began warming up the crowd. This was a cavernous room, little more than a vast empty warehouse. Acoustics were terrible. I could not understand a word coming out of the rows of giant speakers lined up the full length of one wall. The crowd seemed to "get it," however, responding with laughter, cheers and shouts. Oh well, I wasn't alone as no one around me seemed to be responding either. Peering through tiny gaps in the crowd I could perceive movement. Soon a drum roll and cymbals announced something was happening. Then, the strains of the national anthem arose from what was apparently a local high school band. The crowd seemed to be facing one way and many had hands over their hearts. Good heavens, were they pledging allegiance to a Rubio-for-President banner? Dave pointed and I strained to see. Ah...yes, there was a tiny corner of an American flag peeking out around a man's hat. I joined in. The song ended and the band members filed out. Why didn't they stay and play some more?

Nothing happened as more minutes passed.

"I'll give him until 7:45 and we're leaving," I warned Dave. He smiled in agreement.

Precisely at that time, an electricity raced through the crowd and loud chants went up. Rubio, Rubio, Rubio, amid whistles and cheers. "Where is he?" I asked, feeling envious of the small children sitting on their father's shoulders in front of me. Dave pointed. Stretching and weaving I managed to find a small peep hole through the mass of bodies. And there he was! The candidate, in the flesh, dressed in a dark suit, white shirt and red tie, waving outstretched arms and grinning broadly. He wasn't on stage, as I expected, but was standing in the center on some kind of platform. He began his speech, turning around, this way and that, to take everyone in. By now I had removed my hearing aids and put them in my pockets, thus getting rid of the roaring cacophony they create. (Don't believe the commercials. Even the most expensive aids, which I have, will not filter out the reverb of crowd noise.) I could make out a few words, now and then, such as constitution, conservative and Hillary. I could guess the rest. The crowd seemed to react at appropriate times.

"Can you understand it?" I asked Dave.

"Not much," he said.

After about fifteen minutes we agreed to leave. We had seen enough. "But, how do we get out of here?" I asked, gesturing toward the throng behind us.

"Right through there," he pointed to my left. It was the closest way to open space. And so I started. "Excuse me, excuse us," I repeated and the people parted, allowing us through. Our vacated spaces filled up instantly. A pipe-like barrier separated the edge of the crowd from a makeshift side-aisle. I ducked under it, on hands and knees. Dave casually raised the pipe and walked through. I struggled upright, and we were free. We circled way out around the crowd, back behind the media stand toward the tables and the outer barn doors. Surprisingly, once we got away from the mass of people we could see the senator better. Also, when I passed in front of a loud-speaker, I could hear as well. And so, we stayed there leaning up against the wall and watched the rest of the speech.

Happily, I could now see and hear it all. Marco was great! He had the crowd in the palm of his hand, speaking totally without notes. Oh sure, he gives that speech three times a day, and yet he manages to make each time sound like the first time. Indeed, it was both moving and inspiring. He told the heart-breaking story of his parents' struggle in Cuba, and then coming, at last, to the States. The two of them worked hard in a hotel, as a bartender and a maid, for ten years until they could buy their own home and raise their family, able to provide a better life so their kids could experience the American dream.

Marco finished law school with $100,000 in student loans on his back. He understands what that is like and has already proposed detailed, sensible plans to help students.

He spoke eloquently about how each of us, as parents, want the American dream for our children, and what it is going to take for that to happen. He has strategies and expectations and made promises to us, concluding with an eloquent appeal for our vote.

He had the crowd cheering wildly at the end. No need to rise. They were already on their feet.

Dave and I hurried for the door, among the first lucky ones to escape. We found our car with no trouble and made our way off the grounds rather quickly. Dave turned up the heaters, pointed the car north and soon we were out of the city, heading homeward on US 131.

We arrived home in time to reach our rocking chairs and catch John Roberts, the Fox News journalist, making his report from "Grand Rapids, Michigan, with the Rubio campaign."

We held hands, nodded and agreed, "We were there, weren't we?"

(One year later: Note: As it turned out Senator Rubio was forced to drop out of the campaign before the State of Michigan held their primary election. And so we were not afforded the opportunity to vote for him. While he had pledged to resign as a senator, he later relented and "bowed to public demand." He ran again for US Senator from Florida and won that election. Donald Trump went on to win the Republican candidacy and later became President of the United States.)

Editor's Note: The following excerpt is a complete story condensed from The Savage Surrogate, by Dorothy May Mercer, available on MercerPublications.com. It is a serious adult drama, suitable for older teens and up. Rated PG 13.

(Pgs. 17. Approximate reading time: 25 minutes)

Baby Joy

Washington D.C.

United States Senate Hearing Room

"The hearing will come to order," Mike announced, breaking up the small knots of people, who were sipping coffee and speaking in low tones.

"This committee will present evidence of the legal and ethical morass of commercial surrogacy in the United States and extending beyond our borders," Mike continued. "Until now, only six states in the union have a mishmash of laws regulating a business estimated at three billion dollars annually. Other states have looked the other way, a few governors have vetoed bills on principle, and two others specifically outlaw the practice. Until recently, our own District of Columbia imposed a $10,000 fine plus one year imprisonment, although there is now legislation pending to make it legal in the district.

This committee's purpose will be to investigate the industry, with its myriad laws, practices, and abuses, pointing toward the end of drafting model legislation for governing the industry.

"You have in your possession a collection of papers written by experts in the field, and a comprehensive report generated by our own investigating staff. I trust you will take time to digest those findings." Mike looked up with a rueful smile, taking in the empty places.

"The chair understands your time constraints and therefore we will make these hearings as interesting and as swift as possible. In order to speed things along we have sent inquiries to your attention, in advance of this hearing, suggesting that you write out your questions and submit them to me. I will read the questions to our witnesses. A transcript of the questions and testimony will be delivered to your offices. At the end, those senators present may ask additional questions.

Hearing no objection to that procedure, we will call the first witness. Mike stood and shook hands with a young woman who appeared to be very pregnant. She moved to the witness chair, took the oath, and sat behind a microphone.

Mike spoke, "Good morning, Miss. Please tell us your name and why you are here."

"Good morning, senators, and staff members. I am Virginia Gordon. As you can see, I am expecting a baby.

"I am carrying this child for another woman who is unable to have children for physical reasons. She has a genetic disease and is afraid that her babies will inherit the same affliction."

Mike looked at his list of questions. "Thank you, Mrs. Gordon. I will be reading from a list of questions submitted by our committee members. The first inquiry is, please tell us where you live and how you happened to decide to do this."

"With all respect, sir, I'd rather not say where I live, because in my particular state it is illegal to have a surrogate pregnancy. I got into it because I have born three children of my own and this was an easy way to make a good deal of money. My own children had been easy. I mean I wasn't sick with any of them, you know, and I had fairly easy deliveries."

"And has this one been easy for you?"

"No, sir, this one has been completely different. I have been so sick."

"Do you have any idea why?"

"Well, there haven't been any studies, but some think that there may be an incompatibility between the mother and another couple's baby."

"Would you say that there should be more studies?"

"Oh yes. Also, no one knows the long term effects of the injections you have to take."

"Explain that, if you please," said Mike

"Well, I had to take a series of hormone shots to suppress my own ovulation and prepare my uterus for IVF."

"IVF?"

"In vitro fertilization."

"Go on," said Mike.

"Well, you take synthetic estrogen by pill and patch and then inject synthetic progesterone with a huge needle into your butt for six weeks before and after the IVF. It wrecks havoc on your system.

You have to refrain from intercourse with your husband all this time. And then, you go into the lab and lay with your feet up in stirrups while they administer the zygotes by threading a catheter up your cervix and into your womb. Three out of four times, it doesn't take and you have to go through it all again. And you keep self-injecting the hormones into your butt for six weeks, even after the morning sickness kicks in."

By now, several of the younger women in the room had turned pale and one ran out the door, in obvious distress.

"Um," Mike cleared his throat. Turning the paper over and picking up the next sheet he said, "That appears to be the last of our questions, Mrs. Gordon. Do you have anything further to say to this committee?"

"Well, it's just that I think there needs to be more money for research and a federal department to regulate the surrogate industry. There is certain to be more of this in the future, and there is already scandal and corruption in the industry.

"We're not talking about animals here, these are people, real babies and real parents," she said, her voice rising. "When things go wrong, there is untold heartache and chaos. I'm sure you know of some of the lawsuits, with one judge awarding the child to one set of parents and another reversing the order. And nobody cares about the surrogates, now called 'gestational carriers.' It's as if you are just a contractor for service.

"IVF pregnancies seem to generate more medical problems than ordinary pregnancies. Multiple births and premature births are not uncommon. One dangerous condition is called pre-eclampsia, which comes from the infant's blood infiltrating the mother's.

"No one knows the long term effects of the massive injections of hormones. In the case of a defective fetus, the contracts call for an abortion, and that can lead to horrendous problems and lawsuits. Oftentimes the surrogate mother can run up huge hospital bills. The adoptive parents are supposed to pay for this, but they've been known to welch on the deal and leave the woman stuck with ruined credit and a battered body. On the other hand, surrogates have been known to flee to other states to escape their contracts.

"Lawyers and administrators of the clinics and agencies care even less about the babies. There is a lot of money involved and the babies are just a valuable commodity. The whole situation is ripe for fraud and abuse. If there was ever a state of affairs in need of regulation and oversight, this is it, and I hope this committee will step up to the plate. Thank you very much for hearing me out." She nodded at each member and stood.

Mike and the others stood as Mike dismissed her cordially and wished her well.

Cynthia Patterson was pleased with the progress made at the Sub-Committee hearings. After Virginia Gordon's testimony, there were three more witnesses, from differing parts of the United States telling of first hand experiences with notorious court cases and shyster operators. At this point there was no evidence of organized crime activities. The shady operations seemed to be either opportunistic in nature or just plain incompetent.

A Navy wife from San Diego, California testified that she had carried four separate pregnancies to term for an agency in the area.

She told how the surrogate business thrives around military bases, because it is a great way for military wives to make money while their husbands are overseas.

The contracts, which are written by attorneys for the agencies, tended to favor one side more than the other. The fee for the surrogate's service can run from

$75,000 to $125,000, plus the medical and hospital costs. Another popular feature of benefit to the prospective buyers is that military wives are covered by government health insurance, thus sparing the buyer a great deal of money.

******

Cynthia had a particular interest in the hearings because of her eldest sister, Ethel Goodrich who had fallen victim to the program.

Somewhere in the Western United States

Cynthia's sister, Ethel, and husband Nate Goodrich had been unable to have children. After years of trying, Ethel was in her late thirties, when she finally conceived. The two of them were thrilled and could not resist telling everyone right away. Ethel was getting along beautifully with no morning sickness at all, until one day she started passing blood. Her doctor admitted her to the hospital in an attempt to stop it, but it was impossible. The baby miscarried. Ethel was heartbroken beyond comfort. Nate tried to console her, but he was suffering, too.

It was necessary to do a D & C, and during the course of this procedure, suspicious cells were discovered. A biopsy was ordered, which disclosed cancer. Fortunately, it was in an early stage. Three doctors met with the unhappy couple to discuss their options. The only way to be absolutely sure that the cancer was completely gone would be to remove all of Ethel's reproductive organs.

Ethel wept. "No, no, no," she sobbed, shaking her head. "I'll do anything, chemotherapy, or whatever, but please, don't take away my uterus."

183

In the end, Nate won out. He couldn't risk losing his wife. Ethel underwent the surgery.

The results were as good as could be expected, as the surgeons were ninety-nine percent certain they got all the cancer. An added bonus was they were able to save some of her eggs, for possible future fertilization with Nate's sperm.

"It can be very costly," her primary care physician told them later, "but if you and Nate consent, I can refer you to a company that will complete the lab work and freeze and store the embryos for you."

"But, I don't understand," said Ethel. "How can I carry a baby, now?"

"Well, you don't, my dear. There are women who will carry it for you. The company and its agency has people who contract to serve as surrogates. Once the child is delivered, it becomes yours. You are the genetic and legal parents."

Nate smiled at his wife. "Let's at least have the embryos saved. We can do that much. There will be time later to decide whether we want to go through with the rest."

And so they did.

It took the couple three long years to save up enough money for the service, by scrimping and saving every dime and borrowing all they could. They even took out a second mortgage on their house and borrowed on their life insurance policies.

They researched several agencies, consulted with an attorney, and finally selected, not the cheapest, but the one they thought was the best, the most upright, and honest and the one with the best record of results.

A surrogate mother was interviewed and selected. This particular agency believed in having the mother bond with the prospective parents, and so Ethel and Nate were able to follow and enjoy the pregnancy, step by step.

Ethel's girl-friends threw her a baby shower. The surrogate mother attended. Ethel and Nate spent weeks getting everything ready, shopping and fixing up their daughter's room. Truthfully, the baby's prospective Aunt Cynthia had trouble not buying everything in sight. The baby would have her own nursery with all the latest brand new paraphernalia.

Ethel spent many hours in the nursery room just playing with all the cute little girlie outfits and baby things. Cynthia made the cross-country trip, twice, to share in her sister's joyful preparations.

At last, a beautiful baby girl was born by a normal delivery. Ethel and Nate were in seventh heaven. They journeyed to the hospital where they could look at their baby. She was perfect. Their happiness knew no bounds. Grandparents came, as well, during visiting hours. None were allowed to hold her, as yet. They could pick her up and take her home in six days.

Ethel tried to stay busy during the wait. She sent out birth announcements to the newspaper and to friends and relatives. It showed the baby's picture, only hours old. She and Nate had decided on a name, Joy Alice.

The night before the big day, Ethel barely slept from excitement and Nate was almost as bad. Ethel packed everything she could possibly need to bring the baby home, a little outfit, receiving blanket, warm blanket, diapers and a changing mat. She even had a warm bottle of formula, just in case.

Nate took the day off from work, had the car washed and serviced, installed the baby's car carrier in the back seat of the car. When he brought the car around for Ethel, she was more than ready. Nate snapped a picture as she left the house and one more after he seated her in the car. What a great smile! Nate would look at it, again, month's later, and realize it was the last smiling picture he had of Ethel.

Driving to the hospital, Nate observed the speed limit and drove with as much care as if Joy Alice was already in the car. He let Ethel off at the door and drove to a nearby parking space. Ethel waited for him to join her and together they took the elevator up to the birthing floor. Leaving the elevator, they walked directly to the nursery window to look in on their baby. She was not in her bassinet, so they assumed that the nurses were making final preparations for the baby's release to her parents.

Ethel and Nate stepped to the nurses' station.

"Hello, may I help you?" asked the duty nurse.

"Yes, please, we are here to pick up our baby girl," they both beamed.

"And your names?" asked the nurse.

"We are the Goodriches, Nate and Ethel."

The nurse silently tapped into her computer. "Goodrich, you say?"

"Yes, G-o-o-d-r-i-c-h, Goodrich, Nathan and Ethel Goodrich."

The nurse typed some more and gazed at the computer. "And the date of birth?"

"Just six days ago, the nineteenth. She was born at 7:59 P.M."

"I don't see a Goodrich. What was your doctor's name? I'll look under that."

"Dr. Yarnoka, I believe," said Nate.

"Yes, that's right," Ethel confirmed. They grinned at each other.

"Yes, he is a regular here," said the nurse. Let me try Yarnoka… ah… here is his record. He had three deliveries that day. Reinhardt, that was a boy, then another boy. They have both been discharged. Let me see, there was one girl, seven pounds, four ounces, a good weight for a newborn girl. Let's see, she lost weight for the first three days and then she started to gain, which is good. Her mother named her Sally. I like that. Sally Miller."

Ethel wanted to scream, *Will you just shut up! Get to the point!* Instead, she tried to remain calm. "We would like to take our daughter home, now, if you please."

"Well, I don't see any Goodrich here. Let me look a day forward and back. Sometimes these records get misplaced by one day, especially if it is close to midnight."

"It wasn't close to midnight," said Nate, impatiently. Try 7:59 P.M. There can't be many at that exact time, can there?"

"Well, there was just the one, the baby girl Sally Miller was born at the exact same time, 7:59 P.M. on the nineteenth. Are you sure your baby was born at that time?"

Ethel's body started to shake. She felt sick to her stomach.

"Are you feeling all right?" asked the nurse. "You look a little pale. It's only been six days since you delivered. Maybe you should lie down."

Nate held his wife up. "Where is Sally Miller?" he demanded.

"Why, at home, I presume. She was discharged with her mother two days ago."

Ethel crumpled in Nate's arms.

"My wife has fainted!" Mike exclaimed. "Get us some help immediately."

When Ethel woke up, she was staring at pale green curtain dividers and a white ceiling. She saw Nate standing beside her, holding her hand. She turned her head toward him and moistened her lips. He merely looked at her with tears in his eyes.

"What happened?" she asked.

"You fainted."

"I mean what happened to our Baby Joy?"

"She's g-gone. Darling, I'm so sorry."

"Gone? How can she be gone?"

"The surrogate kidnapped her."

"Oh, dear God! No. She can't do that."

"She can and she did," Nate choked.

Ethel merely stared, unable to grasp what happened.

"The police have been alerted," Nate continued, trying to stem his own tears, "but, on the phone, they were not encouraging. They will try to find her, but, even if they do, we must get a Court order to try and get her back. The laws of this state are murky on the subject. We will need to hire our own private investigator and attorney."

"What about the agency? We have a contract," she wailed.

"I called them immediately. They were very sympathetic, but they said that their hands are tied. Apparently, there is no law in this state that protects the new parents. Over the years, law enforcement has stayed out of these disputes.

"It seems, if the birth mother chooses, she can keep the baby."

"Why weren't we told?" she sobbed.

Nate had no answer. The two of them were devastated. They could only hold each other and grieve.

At length, Nate signed for Ethel's discharge. They left the hospital, in sorrow, and went home, empty and forlorn.

Together they pulled the shades in Joy's room and closed the door, permanently. Ethel cried her eyes dry that day and night. Nate comforted her as long as he could and finally fell asleep in exhaustion.

During the weeks that followed, Ethel moved through her days like a zombie. She had left her job to stay home with the baby, and now she was lost. Nate gradually recovered. He had his work to keep him engaged, and there were the police and costly lawyers, keeping him busy with attempts to recover Baby Joy. At length, he had to file suit, naming the agency and the birth mother. Nate's savings were exhausted and the bills mounted exponentially.

Ethel and Nate were barely able to communicate. He tried to bring her into the discussions over the lawsuit, but she had given up hope, entirely. Whenever he brought up the subject, her tears flowed so badly, that he could not stand it.

Nate was receiving news from his private investigator about the baby's progress, but Ethel showed no interest. Eventually, he gave up trying to talk with her about Joy or anything else.

Nate had worn out his friends at work, on the subject. As time passed, the only one who remained interested and sympathetic was his sister-in-law,

Cynthia Patterson. Even Joy's grandparents were tired of listening. They urged Nate to give up the lawsuit and try again with a different surrogate. After all, there were fertilized eggs still frozen, weren't there?

Nate tried to broach that possibility with Ethel. He prevailed upon Cynthia to talk with her, too. Ethel would not hear of it. She dismissed the subject and turned away from both of them, remaining mired in her misery.

Privately, Cynthia thought that Ethel should be seeing a grief counselor. One day she broached the subject with Nate, as they were talking on the phone. He promised to discuss it with Ethel.

At first, Ethel was reluctant, but eventually she agreed to go for group therapy, if Nate would accompany her. Ethel had not left the house in all this time.

The night of their first weekly class, she panicked and braced herself at the door. She couldn't do it. Nate took her arm and gently tried to pull her hands off the doorframe. Ethel started to scream. He had to let go. "Please try," he pleaded.

She shook her head, "I c-can't!"

Nate turned away, got in the car, and went to the class, alone, where he was welcomed. The people gathered in a circle of chairs. They introduced themselves by first names only, and told briefly how they lost a child. Nate had not planned to speak, at all, but when it came around to him, the words began to flow uncontrollably. Nate realized he had found people who understood.

Nate looked forward to the group meetings. Each week he invited Ethel along. She merely shook her head, "No thank you. You go on, Nate."

In time, Nate joined with the group in a restaurant after the meetings. He became acquainted with the members. These were his friends and support group. Once, he stayed behind with two of the women. This became a weekly habit with one woman in particular. Nate hated to go home. As the nightly trysts grew later, Nate let himself into the house quietly and bedded down on the sofa.

As Nate's recovery progressed, he needed to get away from Ethel. He found more and more opportunities to stay out late. She didn't seem to notice. She sat in the same chair staring, most of the time, now. Nate had just about given up fixing her meals. Hours later, the same food remained untouched. She had stopped bathing and fixing her hair. After seeing her in the same clothes, day and night, Nate would lead her into the bedroom and help her change into fresh things.

Nate couldn't afford to hire help for Ethel. At this point he was doing the laundry, cooking and cleaning. The day came when Ethel seemed unresponsive, almost catatonic. Nate made an appointment with their family doctor. When the day arrived, he cleaned her up as best he could and carried her to the car. She said nothing and made no objection.

Nate remained in the waiting room while the doctor examined Ethel. After exhausting every magazine available, Nate went to the window and asked what was taking so long.

"I'll go and check for you," said the receptionist.

Nate waited. When she returned, she told Nate that the doctor had ordered some tests. "I think they will be finished, soon. If you'll just take a seat, someone will call you when she is ready."

After more time had passed, a nurse called, "Mr. Goodrich?"

"Yes," Nate looked up.

"The doctor will see you, now. Come with me, please." She held a clipboard in one arm and opened the door for Nate with the other. "Right this way, please."

Nate followed her down a series of corridors to the very end and into a comfortable office overlooking a small pond and garden.

"Hello, Mr. Goodrich," said the doctor. "If you will just have a seat, please."

This procedure was curious. Nate perched on the edge of a leather bound office chair, and gazed directly at the doctor. What was happening? Nate was sure that nothing could faze him, now, but his palms started to perspire.

"Nate, I've been your doctor for how many years, now? We've been through a lot, haven't we?"

Nate nodded, wishing the doctor would just say it.

"I'm sorry, but I'm afraid I have some bad news."

Nate's heart raced. He wiped his palms on his pants.

"There's no other way to say it, Nate. Your wife's cancer has returned."

Nate paled. His mouth dropped open. "Uh…" he exhaled and fell back in the chair.

The doctor waited.

Nate's brow furrowed. "But… I thought… they got it all."

"I'm sorry, Nate. A few cells escaped. With the deep depression that Ethel has experienced, her body stopped fighting."

"You mean…?"

"No one knows, but I think the cancer has metastasized."

"Spread...?"

"I'm sorry."

"But, what can we do?"

"Well, I'd like to send her to a specialist. There is always hope."

"What are the chances, doctor?"

"That is impossible to say, but I'm certain that without treatment, she doesn't have long."

Nate stared.

"Maybe a few weeks, maybe less. I can't say."

"How soon can we get in to a specialist?"

"Normally, several weeks, but I have a friend who may do us a favor."

"Call him."

"Well, I'd be happy to, but without the patient's consent..."

"What do you mean, doctor? Consent?"

"Ethel adamantly refused to go, Nate."

Nate shook his head sadly. This was the final blow. He lost his baby, his savings, now his wife.

"Do you think you could talk her into it, Nate?"

"I don't know, I doubt it."

"She wants to die, Nate."

Nate drew a deep breath. "Well... I guess I'll take her home. Go ahead and make the appointment. I'll see if I can get her there." He rose and offered a hand to the doctor, who now looked almost as defeated as Nate felt.

The doctor rose and took Nate's hand. "God bless you, son," he said.

"Thank you, doctor... for everything."

******

As time went on, Ethel lost all interest in life. She stopped leaving her bed. Nate could no longer care for her adequately. He called Hospice for help. A kind volunteer visited, daily at first, and then more frequently. Gently she prepared Nate for the inevitable.

Cynthia took some vacation time and flew out to be with her sister and help Nate. In the end, Ethel passed, peacefully.

Nate continued with the therapy group, for a time. They helped him through his new grief. One of the divorced women volunteered to carry one of Nate and Ethel's preserved embryos and help raise the baby herself. Nate thought long and hard about this. At last, he decided against it and ordered the eggs destroyed.

This all happened several years ago. For a while, Nate called Cynthia every week. In a way, he wondered whether he and Cynthia might get together. Gradually the calls tapered off. Nate had moved on with his life. Eventually, he met someone, and married again. The couple were happily looking forward to their second child.

Cynthia realized that, someday, she might need to share some of this story with Mike and his committee. For now, it was part of the past. What remained was a determination to do what she could about the unfair laws. Now with Mike's committee holding hearings on the matter, she had the opportunity.

To continue reading or listening to the exciting novel, *The Savage Surrogate*, by Dorothy May Mercer, please go here:
http://MercerPublications.com/savagesurrogatethe

About the Author-Dorothy May Mercer

Dorothy May Mercer
Author and Creator

Best selling author, Dorothy May Mercer, lives in Michigan, USA, "The Great Lakes State." Taking advantage of its many inland lakes, she and her husband have two homes situated on lakefronts. Not surprisingly, her hobbies include boating, swimming, fishing and just gazing at the water while she conjures up her next thriller. The couple loves to travel, having visited the fifty United States, eight Canadian provinces, Australia, the Caribbean Islands, and Africa, which scenes spice up her novels.

(Pgs. 9. Approximate reading time: 12 minutes)
Excerpt by Dale L. Williams, M.D.

Second Thoughts
Dale L. Williams, M.D.

Jonas Kolbeck was having second thoughts about this whole African idea. What the hell was he doing, trying to be a missionary? He seldom went to church except at Christmas and, sometimes, Easter.

Here he was, thousands of miles from home, flying to a place he had only read about and where no one knew him. The closer he came to his destination, the more the idea of serving in the mission field for a year seemed ridiculous.

Jonas sighed and shifted about in his seat. He couldn't turn back now. His family and friends, excited about his going to Africa to work with the refugees, had given him a big farewell reception at the church in Tipponville. Besides, he knew he was tired and figured the self-doubts would be gone by morning.

Jonas moved again. His back muscles ached from the plane ride. So far, he had been sitting for eighteen hours on the two flights from New York to Kenya in the crowded tourist section. The small Sabena seats were positioned too close together for his six foot three frame and, despite struggling through a number of positions, he could never seem to find one that was comfortable. Making it worse was the elderly, overweight lady in the next seat who was overflowing into his area. Her warm body pressed against him for much of the trip. Also, she apparently had an overactive bladder, requiring frequent visits to the bathroom. Standing awkwardly to allow her to wiggle out each time, made sleep impossible for Jonas. To top it off, a small child in the row behind him kept kicking the back of Jonas's seat, while complaining all the time of being bored.

Feeling the need to use the bathroom, Jonas walked to the back and waited in line. Standing in the aisle, he watched the movie. He was amused as the characters mouthed words, raced cars and shot each other in silence.

The line moved forward and Jonas was in front when a small boy ran up and pulled on the locked bathroom door.

"Son, there's someone in there," Jonas said. "You have to wait your turn."

The boy remained at the door, moving quickly from foot to foot. As the bathroom door opened and a woman came out, Jonas, noticing the small wet spot on the front of the boy's pants, said, with a laugh, "Son, why don't you go in first?"

In the bathroom, Jonas looked into the mirror and was satisfied with his appearance. His brown hair on a well-shaped head was now mussed He needed a haircut. His smile, with almost perfect teeth, was his best feature. The nose was perhaps too prominent and the right eye was slightly smaller than the left. As a child, the nose, inherited from his father, had not bothered him but the difference in his eyes had been a problem. He opened the left eye wide. Now the eyes matched but the eyebrow was too high. Amused, he finished drying his hands.

Standing in the aisle, Jonas attracted the attention of a stewardess who asked if he needed anything. He motioned silently with his head toward the sleeping woman, now occupying almost half of his seat.

The stewardess smiled understandingly. "Would you like another seat?"

"Yes, that would be nice."

The plane finally landed in Nairobi and Jonas waited among the noisy airport crowd for the local mission representative to appear. He looked at his instructions where the name, Martha Kwinga, was written. A vendor came up and tried to interest Jonas in some sausages. He shook his head. As he lingered, other vendors and taxi drivers, in broken English, came up to offer their services, ranging from wood carving and watches to ladies of the night. Finally giving up on the representative, Jonas took a taxi to the hotel.

Checking in, Jonas was given a room on the fifth floor. Looking out the window, he gazed down on a hodgepodge of buildings, some modern and tall, others small and obviously old.

The sounds from the street merged with the rumbling of the air-conditioner that emitted a lingering odor of smoke The room was painted light green with a single bed and small cabinet against one wall, opposite a picture of giraffes. The adjoining bathroom had a simple shower stall.

He felt disorientated because of the time change. According to his watch, it was early in the afternoon in Kenya, but the middle of the night in Wisconsin. He would have liked to take a nap but knew it was important to put off sleeping as long as possible in order to adjust to the new time zone. He decided to stretch his legs and walk around the downtown.

Jonas strolled the streets taking in the sights of this unique city. The guidebook had described Nairobi as a combination of European and African cultures. This was evident on Mama Ngina Street. The sidewalk was crowded with Africans, in colorful clothing, mixing with suited businessmen and teenagers in jeans and casual dress. He overheard bits of conversations in English, French and other languages as he passed an outside café. At one of the tables a beautiful black woman with short hair and western dress was in earnest conversation with a blond man who kept nodding in a bored manner.

The buildings were a jumble of the different cultures. His hotel, the Hilton, was a modern cement circular structure rising twenty floors high, like the queen on a chessboard. Within the same block was the Hunda Wholesale Bazaar, a square, faded yellow, two-story store selling African trinkets and memorabilia. Jonas casually stopped to look at the window display. The owner, standing outside on the sidewalk, eyed him expectantly.

The short, dark Asian started cajoling, "Mister, you an American?"

Jonas did not answer but the man persisted. "We got wonderful gifts for you to take home for your wife and kids. Look." He pointed towards a large stuffed elephant in the window, "This is a great gift for a boy."

Shaking his head, Jonas began to walk away. He would probably buy presents at the end of his tour so it made no sense to buy and store them for a year. The owner grabbed his arm and gently eased him toward the store, as he kept talking. "I give you a great deal. Fifty percent off everything."

Jonas shrugged his shoulders. "Why not. It's a good way to kill some time."

Once inside, Jonas became enthralled. The aisles were filled to overflowing with colorful paintings, stuffed animals, carvings and other gifts with an African motif.

Incense sticks were burning, clouding the air with a slightly acrid smell. It was like entering a different world--the real Africa.

Jonas was examining a display of beautifully painted gourds when he saw the perfect gift for his niece. It was a shiny necklace of bright red and green stones. Julie loved jewelry and the price was only six hundred shillings.

"Do you take American dollars?" Jonas asked the cashier.

The dark-complexed lady behind the counter, a younger, prettier version of the owner, nodded. "Yes, we take most major currencies."

Jonas handed her a five-dollar bill. She looked at him, "The price is six hundred shillings, that's seven dollars and seventy cents in your money."

"I believe the man outside said I was to get a fifty percent discount."

"One moment, please." The young woman went outside to talk to the older man. Jonas could see the nodding and shaking of heads. The cashier returned, "My father says the discount is for everything except the jewelry."

As he was paying, Jonas's energy began to flag. It was time to return to the hotel. He would have to get some rest for visiting the animal park in the morning.

Jonas ordered room service, took a shower, and then stretched out on the bed. Although exhausted, he felt too keyed up to sleep. He turned on the television. As he watched an old episode of Bonanza, his eyes began to feel heavy. The last thing he remembered was Little Joe riding up to the ranch house and calling out to his brother "Hoss, we're missing some cattle from the back pasture".

The telephone was ringing. Jonas was in surgery and irritated that no one was picking it up. "Will someone answer that damn phone?" he shouted. The loud ringing continued and he suddenly woke up.

Picking up the instrument on the bedside table, he heard, "Doctor Jonas Kolbeck? I'm Martha Kwinga, the local organization's representative. Welcome to Africa. I'm sorry I couldn't meet you at the airport. Was the driver there on time? Are you comfortable at the hotel?"

When she paused for breathe, Jonas slipped in, "No. No. Yes. And, at least I was until the telephone rang."

"Oh, I'm sorry." Her voice went from bouncy to mildly accusatory, "You were sleeping?"

"That's okay. I can get back to sleep. I haven't had a good night's sleep in two days. It's been..."

"You're in luck. There's a flight into Goma tomorrow. Actually I should say today."

The cobwebs were beginning to clear from Jonas's head. "Wait a minute. I thought I had two days in Nairobi."

"Yes, you do, or did, because the plane usually flies into Goma on Wednesdays. Only this week it's going on Monday because some of the United Nations staff needs to get back."

"What time?"

"At 4:30."

"In the afternoon?"

"No. This morning."

Jonas looked at my watch. "That's in four hours. There's no way..."

"The taxi will pick you up outside the hotel at four. I'll see you at the airport."

"Wait a minute..."

She was gone.

When the taxi first arrived at the hotel entrance, Jonas had asked, "How far away is the airport from my hotel?"

The driver shrugged his shoulders, "I don't know. Depends upon the time of day and the traffic. Usually about thirty minutes, but this early in the morning, maybe twenty minutes."

The cab bounced along the highway and, each bump made Jonas Kolbeck more agitated. He opened the passenger window to let in the night air. Although cold and damp against his face, it was a relief from the smell of incense and cigarette smoke that permeated the inside of the van. As they bounced between potholes, Jonas looked out the window at the dark shapes of trees and homes passing swiftly by. His mood became even more grouchy.

He didn't have any idea of what Africa was like. Before this, he had never even been outside of the United States. Looking for change after the death of Molly, Jonas had impulsively signed up for the mission work, partly in response to his sister Barbara's urging. Now he was having second thoughts about volunteering to spend a year as a physician working in a refugee camp in Zaire.

What a crazy idea! More like stupid!

~*~*~*~*~

After returning from Michigan where Molly was buried, Barbara tried to draw her brother out of his morose silence. "Jonas, what are you going to do now?"

Jonas shook his head, continuing to look out the side window. He was remembering their last conversation. If only he had been home on time, both Molly and his daughter might still be alive.

Jonas had to admit that Barbara adjusted to the tragedy better than he did. He remembered the one Sunday afternoon, about a month ago, when she came over to Jonas's new apartment. She chatted with him about the family but he was not paying much attention.

Exasperated, she demanded, "For crying out loud, Jonas, how long do you intend to sit around feeling sorry for yourself?"

"What?" She had his attention.

"You heard me. You need to go to work and quit moping around."

Jonas shrugged his shoulders, not answering. He wished she would go away.

Barbara persisted. "Everyone misses Molly, but I can imagine what she would say about your martyr act."

"It's not an act." Now Jonas was angry.

She nodded, "Of course it is. You're not the first person to lose a spouse. Others get on with their lives."

"I know that but ..." Jonas was on the defensive.

Barbara interrupted, "She's been gone now for four months and all you've done since that time is feel sorry for yourself. It's time to grow up and get a life."

Jonas glared at his sister. "Perhaps Molly dying has something to do with it."

"Maybe. Anyway, ask yourself, would Molly want you act this way? I don't think so."

"I don't care," Jonas snapped. "I can't help how I feel."

"Of course you can. Here," Barbara showed him a church publication about the massacres and suffering in Rwanda and Zaire. "If you think you are miserable, read this."

"No thanks." Jonas threw the church publication on the coffee table.

That night, as he watched television, Jonas's eyes strayed to the magazine. He picked it up. It was full of pictures and the description of different refugee groups around the world. On the last page were ads asking for volunteers for their missionary programs. One, for physicians in the refugee camps of Africa, caught his eye. On an impulse he contacted New York.

And now was on his way to Goma in this awful taxi.

~*~*~*~*~*~

Editor's Note: If you enjoyed reading this excerpt, we recommend the complete story about Jonas' hair-raising adventures in Africa, "Remember How Much I Love You." Go Here: http://amzn.to/2vEmYVV

or Here:

http://mercerpublications.com/rememberiloveyou.html

About the Author-Dale L. Williams, M.D.

Dr. Dale L. Williams, M.D grew up on a dairy farm in Michigan with his parents, two sisters and one brother.

He worked full-time, earning his education by cleaning offices, factory work, tutoring, working at a grocery store and for eight years as an orderly at mental hospitals.

Dale served in the U.S. Army, stationed for two years in Berlin. While in Germany he met and married his beautiful wife Christel who has, since, blessed him with three fine sons and one lovely daughter.

He studied at Eastern Michigan University, The University of Munich, *Frei Universitat* in Berlin, earning Bachelors degrees, and then his doctorate at Wayne State University. Later he earned an MBA from the University of South Florida.

After graduating from medical school, he spent one year at the Pingtung Children's Hospital in Taiwan for

World Vision of California. He established a pharmacy at the hospital and developed outpatient clinics in mountain villages.

Dr. Williams' compelling second novel, "Remember How Much I Love You," was inspired by his extensive service as a medical missionary in Africa. The events as described in the book came from listening to the horror stories told him by his patients. Dr. Williams maintains that the truth is even worse than those events he fictionalizes in the book. His experiences included work in a hospital in Niger, in a Zaire refugee camp, building schools and medical clinics in Rwanda and–his very worst experience–serving in Ethopia during the famine.

Dale's medical missionary experience has taken him to hot spots all over the world. While working in China to help set up hospitals, he visited students who were demonstrating in Tiananmen Square. He escaped just two days before the tanks rolled in. Other posts were in Haiti, Israel, Lebanon, El Salvador, Guatemala, Mexico, Nicaragua, and Taiwan.

For thirty years, Dr. Williams was a managing partner of a private practice in family medical care, in Muskegon, Michigan. At the same time, he was instrumental in setting up The Koinonia Clinic serving the poor in that area.

Due to his wide experience and expertise, Dr. Williams is in great demand. His credentials, certifications, positions, memberships, and titles read like a Who's Who. He has served as officer for prestigious medical societies, academies, boards, banks and city councils.

It hasn't all been about medicine. He has been chairman for Clean Water, Michigan's Martin Luther

King Day, and Synergy International. Also, he has been very active in his church, instrumental in founding at least one new church.

One wonders how he finds time to polish his golf game, or read a book, much less write one. As the saying goes, "If you want something done, give it to a busy person." Dale L. Williams M.D. is a mighty busy person. We hope he finds time for more works like this one.

A Visit in Heaven with Princess Diana and Fr. Bob Murray

Channeled By Marcia McMahon, M.A.

May 2017

(Editor's Note: As this is happening, Marcia is preparing to host the Peaceful Planet show, with guest Fr. James Murray.)

Marcia speaks:

Calling in Father Bob Murray, calling in Princess Diana and all the major guides to be present with James and I, whom we have on the show this evening. We intend to make it fun and uplifting.

Fr. Bob: This is Father Bob. We've been trying to connect to you all week and were glad you finally took some time out from your cleaning and other activities to spend some time in the heavenly realms. Now if you'll just let go of all your expectations for this evening Marcia, for you are a perfectionist and you're too hard on yourself. You need to be easier on yourself and things will go easier for you in general.

Fr. Bob continues: I can't tell you how proud I am of my son James and how good he's really getting at receiving my messages accurately.

Marcia: Well Father Bob, if I may say so, you are a great channel and a great teacher so that leaves nothing out of the equation! There isn't any room for error is there? LOL.

Fr. Bob: When too much rain or inclement weather affects you it does affect the mood, so all of you out there who have been feeling a little bit of the blues lately, it's to be attributed much to the weather.

Stay connected to the silver cord as you relax and release more and more of your cares and worries. See yourself enveloped in a force field of white light. You are in a long tube where no negative entities can attach to you as you travel through the silver cord all the way over to my house. Count one, two, three and you're going to land right at the gate to the property. You will open the gate yourself and come up the red-brick lined walk. There are flowers all over on both sides of the walkway, decorating the front of the house and inside of the house as well.

So you're going to gently knock and I'm going to welcome you into the study.

Fr. Bob: Come on in Marcia and sit down. It's a long time since you've paid me a visit.

Marcia: I'm happy to be here.

Fr. Bob: Well, what can I get you?

Marcia: Oh the red wine looks good or maybe whatever else you have in the way of tea or coffee.

Fr. Bob: Well, make up your mind!

Marcia: I'll have half a glass of red wine, no more. Thank you Bob.

Fr. Bob: So just sit down and make yourself at home. I'm here with the animals at my feet. I'm on my comfortable chair as you can see. You can observe my writing implements as you saw them last time. So anyway it's been my understanding that Diana is anxious to meet you in person and would like to shake your hand. She has something she wants to tell you.

So in my formal way of going about things here on the other side, we are going to go over to Diana's Castle and pay the great lady a visit. Are you game for that?

Marcia: Well Bob my heart is going pitter-patter and I'm getting a little nervous at the thought of really meeting Diana. But I've seen her in my dreams before and I've spoken with her almost daily for sixteen years.

Fr. Bob: Yes, well, she has quite a presence you'll soon find out so... yes I'm chuckling a bit. I'm sitting here in my study looking around at the flowers coming up in the Spring. I'm standing by the window looking out, gazing at the Vista that I have. I can see Diana's Castle in the distance!

Marcia: I can see her castle, too.

Fr. Bob: So we'll leave my place here. First, I'll go tell the housekeeper that I will be gone till dinner.

We're going to go out of the front door and walk across the lawn observing all the flowers and just getting into the sensations of the day. We've got a lot of sunshine today and a nice pleasant breeze.

Marcia describes the scene: We're walking up an old kind of dirt road on the way to Diana's Castle and kind of up the meadow. We're walking together, Bob and I. Bob's a pretty good walker and I'm a little bit behind him. But that's all right. I see that the castle is in the distance. It has quite a few different spires and emblems from different time periods. There are large, grey, thick walls and spires on top.

We are coming up to a huge oak wooden door with a huge old-fashioned knocker. There's also a fancy doorbell and a new garage off to the side where they store their various cars.

So here I am!

Bob turns to me and says, "Are you sure you're ready to meet Diana?"

I'm smiling and I'm saying, "Let me take another deep breath!"

I seem to have changed myself into a well-manicured lady. Looking down at myself, I discover that I'm wearing a deep blue indigo dress and fancy shoes and some fancy handmade amethyst jewelry. I feel a little bit insecure about meeting the Diana!

Okay you, Bob, can knock or ring or whatever you do! I suppose the Butler will answer the door right?

Laughing Bob says, "Of course!"

This guy dressed in a suit comes to the door and he asks, "How may I help you?"

Bob says, "We're here by the invitation of her Royal Highness Princess Diana. She is requesting the presence of Marcia in twenty minutes."

The Butler says, "Welcome! Do please step in and I'll make you more comfortable. Would you step to the right and into the Princess's waiting room? I'll call her for you."

So we are stepping into this very elegant room. It looks sort of French Provincial with late 15th Century furnishings. There are floor-to-ceiling windows and plants all around. It is full of light. You can see the spacious surroundings everywhere, in and out. The exterior of the castle has a variety of different flags and emblems, creating a more medieval look. It is simply awe inspiring.

The interior is more light and airy, with a very uplifting vibe. It is filled with antiques. In Diana's living room, there's a big ceiling painting of clouds in the sky and angels, in high baroque style. There are some portraits of the royal family that she keeps as memorabilia and of course up-to-date portraits of Harry, William and Catherine and their children, Charlotte and George. On the opposite wall, hanging right in her living room, I see some of my portraits in watercolor that I've done of Diana. Then we're led into the family room to her studio.

Here she is!

It's very, very touching, as she comes down the stairs, dressed in a pink sort-of suit. As she approaches me she says, "I've been wanting to congratulate you for so many years for your fine peace work with me. I'm so very honored that you've done all this work for no payment and no real thanks from anyone except a few of your closest followers, associates and friends. I so appreciate what you've done for me; as well as my family and of course for the peace of mankind at this time!"

(What a statement, I think!)

I curtsy to Diana, and take her hand. I'm saying, "Oh Your Royal Highness it's my pleasure to finally meet. You're such an angel! And you're so beautiful!" I gaze into her cornflower blue eyes which convey loving warmth and a zeal for life. Her golden hair even has a bit of a halo and she glows, radiant with beauty.

Princess Diana is glowing from head to toe with a pink light in the pink suit. She's got very special earrings on--the pearl earrings she used to like to wear. She doesn't wear the sapphire because that belongs to Catherine now. That was passed on. Nor does she have her sapphire ring But she's got some beautiful pearls and her suit is very light and as airy as springtime. It is almost like a breath of fresh air. Everything smells of roses as she's got pink roses everywhere in the house. The house is homey--more homelike inside than it is outside where it looks more like a castle.

In the living room Diana sits down at the white baby grand piano. She wants to play a musical piece for both of us. Wow, I wasn't expecting all this! The butler is going to bring in some tea and hors d'oeuvres for us. We are actually at the time of high tea, about 2 o'clock in the afternoon. So that's kind of fun.

Bob and I are sitting here in the royal audience hall. I'm looking around at the spectacular wealth. We hear a rumble of children's feet in the hall. There's a back room where they keep all of their toys. Suddenly, here they are, filing into their seats to hear the concert. Outfitted in suits and coats, they look like boarding school children. Diana takes care to invite them in to hear her playing.

So she is welcoming the children into this room and she's going to play one of the songs that John Lennon has done. I guess this is her way of telling me that she really likes Remarkable Diana (written by Bob Murray, lyrics by Marcia in her book, *Notes from John*) and she really likes the Peaceful Planet. So she's going to play both tunes for us on the piano!

And then she's going to play a recording for us to hear of the children's choir as they sing *Make Me a Channel of Your Peace* by St. Francis of Assisi--her favorite song. The choir of children sing along beautifully. She's playing in this beautiful pink suit and there are angel-like beings all around her. Also she's got angels on the wallpaper and statues of angels in her decor in the apartments. Everything I can see sparkles like jewels.

She's even got a little portrait of me and some of her other channels on the wall. She's got a lot of memorabilia as well. She says in her mind to me, "I think of you as family. I want you very much to know how much love I have for you, Marcia; and for all of my channels and all who are doing the good work! I want to especially thank Michele who's done this beautiful work of the videos, and I want to thank Rose and I want to thank Andrew and want to thank Father Murray and James Murray and it's like we all are spiritually united in the cause for peace!"

Diana has a kind of theater that she's can take us to later.

So we are enjoying the tea served by the maid or whatever you would call this wonderful person who is beautiful in every way. The maid is a friend of Diana's who likes to help out with kitchen things and cooking. She is serving us these little cucumber and cress sandwiches. We're having tea with a little honey. It's all quite lovely.

The music ends and then we all clap when it seems the Princess is through playing. And then she says she is going to play another number for us. She is playing an old song *Goodbye England's Rose,* by Elton John. It's making her sad! Tears rolled down my cheeks, and even Father Murray is tearing up. Diana says, "This is to honor my 20th anniversary here in spirit, and all the good that I did!"

Diana then announces, "Brothers and sisters I watch over you, now. Know that the good that you do lives on in heaven, and we are provided a wonderful afterlife.

"I would so want my sons to know about your fine artwork and your fine channeling of me in order to make every effort to get in touch with house of Windsor."

Diana is singing and playing along with the song and it's very somber and very touching. Of course our thoughts go back to Westminster Abbey and her funeral.

The children are seated throughout the entire time Diana plays for us. (I myself have never seen children so well behaved! It must be the spell of Diana and her magic with children.)

And then it's suddenly time to go. The maid comes in, takes the refreshments and the children are standing alert. Diana is going to escort us to the door. *So long, sweet Princess.* She offers her hand and gives me a big hug. And then she offers her hand to Father Murray and gives him a big hug!

I can see tears welling up in Murray's eyes, feel them dropping down my cheeks, and then we go to the door. We are ready to go.

The path is lined with the iris and now the peonies are up as well, just coming up in her magnificent gardens. There are fields of various wildflowers in the distance too. But here there are mostly neatly manicured bushes and a maze, like any royal palace.

We've had more sunshine so I'm happy to say that I'm in a better mood.

We walk back to Fr. Murray's house on that same dirt path. We materialize light raincoats on the way, as it has begun to drizzle.

Now I'm back with Father Bob. I thank him as I fade from the scene finding myself comfortable at my computer in my home looking out from my window on the garden once more!

Excerpt from Marcia McMahon's novelette:

Martha

Introduction. **2015 Notes on my visit to Israel:**

The Early Christian church of Tagba was about less than one mile away from the Mount of the Beatitudes in Galilee. It was very sacred. And the church had loaves and fishes in it and all round. The day I visited that place many memories came alive, flooding back, for me.

I will always treasure my time in Israel as [it is] the most sacred ground, because the Master walked there with men and women a long time ago. It feels like only yesterday as I remember now, more and more. It is as if I am right there again, as Martha, and it is happening now.

Sermon on the Mount – Jesus Heals Many

33 A.D.

I see him in a white robe, I am walking right beside him, walking along on a hillside.

It is about 70 F degrees and the sunshine is all round. He is tall with a white robe. His hair gently falls over his shoulders. He walks surrounded by crowds of people everywhere. Why am I so close to him as if I could even touch him? He smiles and it makes the sunshine so much brighter. His glistening white teeth and handsome looks radiate thru his large blue eyes. His gaze falls far away, although he is with us but seeming somewhere else at the same time. When he

217

moves to speak he uses hand gestures. Like any teacher he must get the students' attention. He raises his hands to get the attention of the big crowd, which is pressing in all round us.

There is a bench set up for healing. I can see Jesuha's face. Large hazel blue eyes, penetrating and dreamy too. When Jesuha looks at you, you can become mesmerized by love in just one instant. He knows love, is love, and emotes unconditional love. With long dark hair, and gleaming white teeth, he is what one would call gorgeous.

He emits a radiance that energetically penetrates the audience.

I have bread I baked this morning. I think we have unusual breads with us that we baked. We knew there would be crowds but since we were on the road I could not possibly bake enough for a crowd that size.

And then a little boat came up and there were fishes, plus more food. The little fishing boat brought about five to ten fish. They were skimpy little red things in a net. I believe it was Peter who had gone to get them, at Jeshua's request.

Oh my, I think, *that pathetic fisherman. Does he think he can feed this size crowd with that many fish?* I ponder.

Jesuha has a way to help the people. He is speaking now. I have come to hear him on the large hillside beside the sea of Galilee. *It is good place for an orator,* I think.

There are many people herding around Jesus. Jesuha is speaking but I have found it hard to hear. "Blessed are the poor in spirit, for theirs is the kingdom of heaven. Blessed are they that mourn for they shall be comforted. Blessed are they that seek after righteousness, for they shall be filled."

[Editor: This would have been the Beatitudes.]

Jesuha is speaking but I cannot hear much due to the crowds.

The day and teaching are spectacular. We are up on a hillside. There are children coming with fevers and many mothers are in tears. He is healing them one by one. He will take each child, gently caress the fevered forehead, and then release that child to his or her mother. The lame stand up, the fevers are all healed within no time.

Women are weeping, down on their knees. Children jump for joy at the sights and sounds. The lines are so long.

I try to bring water to the master. I am afraid he is greatly tired.

The Jews are so loud and cynical after seeing a miracle. Right before their eyes, there is miracle after miracle. And the Jews just scoff and walk away.

We are up on a hillside. There are children coming, with fevers many mothers in tears. He is healing them, each one.

Jesus looks very good looking and when he smiles he lights up the whole world. Mother Mary is there. Some of his friends are there. I see many I know. I recognize Peter, James and his brother. John. Peter is a man's man.

We have Lazarus, our whole group--our little group of disciples. We plan to camp out that night on the hillside.

The Loaves and Fishes

Jesuha created a big stir in the countryside that day. Word got out about his big blessing--the blessing of the loaves and fishes. Word got out concerning the "big blessings". He was always working in miracles, but people liked to embellish his story.

They made it a miracle. No miracle. They all decided to share. He taught all day and many would have had to journey home very hungry. I gave my bread. The basket of fish were given. Jesus stood up in a loud voice and thanked the Father in heaven for feeding his flock. We began to spread out little picnic blankets. Everyone pitched in. The hunger and the joy were so very palpable.

Suddenly hearts were opened, and bottled wine; caskets of wine, little cheeses and honey jars were everywhere. The fish was burning on open campfires. It was a giant picnic. Everyone helped everyone to get enough. Miraculously, there was no shortage. Not even the scrawniest of children went without at least a piece of bread in their mouths. This was to be one of the last journeys with the Master. He told me so later on that day.

"Where I am going you cannot come, Martha. I will never leave you again," he said

Tears filled my eyes. I could not bear to hear it. It went thru me as giant balls of love, pain, and knowing. I could not think about that right now.

~~~~~~

I did not marry in that lifetime.

I had to make many meals for Jesus. Jesus' friends were not very helpful to me. To make all those types of people happy, I did it. I was an organized person fit for the work. I remember where we stayed at other homes in Galilee. I still managed. My sister never did much work.

Mary did sit at the foot of the master, ignoring me. Even Lazarus did not care about the home or the meals. It broke my heart but everyone still expected me to be Martha and make all their meals.

I never got to spend as much time with him as I wanted to because of the expectations that I would do all the cooking and clean up after too. That meant less time with Jesus. I felt heartbroken. I know there is a saying about Mary having taken the "better part," and it's so true. But where would the disciples have been without someone caring about their meals, their clothing and their care? I did the weaving, too. I don't believe they would have made it that far on empty stomachs or without my small part. In fact it is the richness of the lifetime I had with Jesus that made the sacrifice of entertaining strangers all the more satisfying. For this story is like no other in any of my times here on this sweet earth.

It feels like only yesterday as I remember now, more and more.

~`~`~`~

"Martha my child," Jesus said, "I am looking forward to seeing you again. Till we meet again, lo I'm always with you! "

About the Author-Marcia McMahon

Marcia McMahon

BA, Ursuline College

MA, Case Western Reserve University And The Cleveland Institute of Art

Diana Gallery Online:

www.dianaspeakstotheworld.com

Former Show Host, Marcia's Magical Mystical hour on www.spreaker.com www.iheartradio.com. with Sat Night Ride

Show host, Peaceful Planet, www.bbsradio.com, since 2005.

Visit the author/artist for beautiful artwork and reviews,

www.dianaspeakstotheworld.com

or marciadi2002@yahoo.com,

Marcia is an accomplished artist, retired professor of Art History, and Spiritual Teacher.

Marcia teaches **Angelic Awakening** classes to accompany her Reiki practice. She is internationally recognized angel intuitive/psychic and author. Her books are channeled inspiration from Princess Diana about how to create a world of peace and unity. Marcia

is an accomplished Artist and teacher of 30 years was named in Who's Who World for 2007, Who's Who in American Women for 2010. Marcia hosts the Earth Angels for Peace on Yahoo groups and has taught many the way to connect to Spirit . She is known for her show, the highly acclaimed **Peaceful Planet** on www.bbsradio.com. She is a nationally certified Hypnotist with NGH, and does past lives regression, hypnosis for self-esteem and Angelic Reiki. Marcia has overcome stage four breast cancer and remains well today. Marcia's clients range from readings for political figures to coaching with reiki and nutritional counseling. Her books have reached top diplomats and presidents. Marcia works with spiritual realms to bring through clarity and healing on multi-dimensional levels in her writing and consultations. She is the author of *Princess Diana's Message of Peace*, (03), and *With Love from Diana, Queen of Hearts*, published in 2005.Marcia most recent release is titled *Notes from John, Messages from Across the Universe*, detailing the afterlife of the late John Lennon and his urgent request for songs for peace. This was a unified effort with famous medium Robert Murray of Canada. John approached both Bob and Marcia desperately in two different countries at the same time, 2005, with his request for world peace. See http://www.dianaspeakstotheworld.com, www.divineconenctionswithreiki.com.
www.enlightendhypnosis.net
Marcia channels Archangel Michael, and has just released *Ascension Teachings Archangel Michael*. (Released 2012) a new book explaining in clear words the Ascension process and earth changes.
Marcia now hosts her own radio show the **Peaceful Planet on www.BBSradio.com/peacefulplanet.** Her interviews have been heard on hundreds of programs on radio and TV.
Reach Marcia at marciadi2002@yahoo.com

Dreams on My Fingertips
A Read-Aloud Story for Children
Mary Ann Vitale

It was a special occasion, a birthday party for Grandma. Mom wanted her little girl, Karlina, to look beautiful and took her to a beauty salon. The young child looked wide-eyed at the lady who hummed a happy tune as she washed, curled, and put Karlina's hair up in a bun. The lady finished by putting hair spray and sparkles in the child's hair. Karlina looked in the mirror. She was pleased with her new look. "Beautiful!" she thought. "Maybe one day I will be a hair magician." Then, she touched her thumb and said, "I will add this one to my list: Dreams on my fingertips." This was her first experience of getting her hair done. Now, Mom and daughter were ready to leave.

During the party, Grandma read first her granddaughter's funny but thoughtful card: "You may be a year older and going over the hill, but did you live yesterday's dreams? Every day is always a good day to start climbing the hill and looking at the world below."

"Climbing the hill?" Grandma chuckled. "I am too old for hills! Climbing is for young people." Then she looked at the little girl and said, "Karlina, your card talks about my dreams, but do you have any dreams of your own? What would you like to do when you grow up?"

Looking at her thumb, Karlina excitedly answered, "Yes, Grandma! When I grow up, I want to be a ... um ... um ... I want to be a hair magician. I want to cut and curl women's hair and then make a nest on top of their heads. Also, I want to shave their long hair and glue it on men with bald heads."

Grandma asked, "Do you mean a hair beautician?"

"Yes, a hair beautician," answered the little girl.

"Where did you get this idea from?" said Grandma.

"I got it from the beauty shop, when I got my hair done," Karlina answered.

"Is that all you want to do?" Grandma asked.

"I have many dreams, one for each finger," answered Karlina. She pointed at her second finger and said "I want to be a face painter so I can paint my eyes blue and put red lipstick all over my lips."

"You mean a make-up artist?" asked Grandma.

"Yes, a make-up artist." Karlina answered.

"Tell me the rest of your dreams," Grandma said.

Lifting her third finger, Karlina said, "I would love to be a math magician so I can call the attendance, teach children how to count with their fingers, and sing the ABCs!"

"I think you mean a mathematician or a math teacher," said Grandma.

"Yes, a math teacher," the child agreed.

Then Karlina looked at her fourth finger, "One day I will be a singer, just like the Wiggles, and sing all the beautiful songs, like a bird in the air. I promise you will see me on TV!"

The girl touched her fifth finger and said, "I also want to be a nurse like my mommy and work in a 'hapsitibol,' then give shots to sick people so they can get better."

"You mean a "hospital?" Grandma corrected.

"Yes, a hospital," said the little girl.

Again, Karlina looked at her other hand, the sixth finger and said, "I think it would be nice to be a fairy, like the one in 'The Water Lily Fairy' book, so I can give candy, chocolate, and gold coins to all the children. Then, I can touch a frog with a wand and turn him into a prince."

"Is there anything else?" Grandma asked.

Karlina looked at her fingers, touching the seventh one, "Yes, Grandma, I have many more. I want to be the first woe-man resident and give out free ice cream every day to all the kids and I will let them stay home from school and play!"

"You mean the first woman-president?" asked Grandma proudly.

"Yes," said the child, "the first woman-president."

On the eighth finger, Karlina said, "I also want to be a mommy, so I can give a bottle of milk to the baby, change her diaper, put baby powder all over her cute little toes and tickle her belly to make her laugh."

"Grandma, the ninth finger is my favorite. I want to be an artist with a brush and paint the world in many colors. I would make a beautiful flower for my mommy and hang it on the wall."

Grandma said, "I see you have many dreams for when you grow up."

The child looked at her tenth finger and said, "Wait, Grandma, I have one more dream saved, just for you, the best one! I want to be a real magician so I can play a trick for you and make you my age, so we can play together. You will look in the mirror and I will say 'Now, you see me. Now, you don't.' "

Grandma looked at the little girl with a wistful look and said, "I love the dreams you have for when you grow up, but, right now, you are young. You have lots of time before you decide what to do."

Mom interrupted, "Let's not tire Grandma, dear. Now, let's open the presents and have cake and ice cream before it melts." While eating the cake, the child licked her fingers and said, "Grandma, what do you want to do when you grow up?"

Smiling, Grandma replied, "I want to keep you this small so I can have you a little longer for myself." With tears in her eyes, she hugged the little girl.

Grandma, Mom, and Karlina enjoyed the rest of the party.

At the end, as they were leaving, Grandma waved at them, thinking, "I really wonder what she is going to be one day!"

Karlina left with many ideas on her mind. She looked at her ten fingertips and as she sat quietly in her car seat, she thought sleepily, "Which dream should I choose when I grow up?"

Copy and content editor: Sisa Colletti Vanelli

About the Author--Mary Ann Vitale

Mary Ann Vitale

Mary Ann Vitale is a bilingual, Amazon Best Selling award-winning author of children's books. Her first published book, The Water Lily Fairy is the winner of the 2013 YATR Literary Awards Best Children's Book. Her recent book, The Street Where the Dollar Tree Grew is the winner of the 2014 LSOR Reviewers Choice Awards. She is married and has three grown children. She loves spending quality time with her eight grandchildren, teaching them the wonderful traditions learned from her heritage.

Mary Ann never dreamed of writing children's books. The language barrier was a challenge to her writing career. She was born in Sicily. As a young child, she always loved books, even though they were not available. At a young age, she moved to the U.S.A. She attended Cosmetology School and college. She is fluent in the Italian, Sicilian, and English languages. At the age of fifty, she wrote her first story for children. Urged by constant inspiration, she wrote many other stories and poems. One day, she woke up with the realization "a writer was born!" Mary Ann has always kept in close contact with her inner child. (See more here)

These are her published books: *The Water Lily Fairy, La Fata delle Ninfee (The Water Lily Fairy,* Italian version), *The Water Lily Fairy at the Ice Cream Palace, La Fata delle Ninfee al Castello del Gelato (The Water Lily Fairy at the Ice Cream Palace,* Italian version), *Ants In My Pants,* Formiche Sui Miei Jeans (Ants In My Pants, Italian version), *Mommy, Where Does Tiger Live?, Julie and Her Seven Calves, Mouse Goes to the Doctor, The Street Where the Dollar Tree Grew,* and *Fingerprints on the Mirror.* Recently she published two coloring books, *Fingerprints on the Mirror, The Coloring Book* and *The Water Lily Fairy, The Coloring Book.* Her books will be available in five different languages: English, Italian, Sicilian, French, and Spanish.

Please go here for Mary Ann Vitale's Amazon page: US: http://amzn.to/2vvefkd

UK: http://amzn.to/2gb42r4

Little Gems
Nancy S. Calumet

On good authority
I understand our Soul
leaves the body before death
so if a person dies in battle
there is no pain

Rest your fears
your loved one suffered not

Who will guide your Soul to Heaven
Whomever you imagine

Your thoughts are things
if you picture being met by Jesus
so it will be

Often times it will be an angel or
a faithful Spirit Guide who accompanies
us on our journey home

White Eagle says all the pets we have cared
for and thought lost will be the first to greet us
followed by friends and family

We may spend some time in a hospital or infirmary
depending on the state of our mind and body
when we cross over

If you die of old age you know
old age ain't for sissies
as Betty Davis once said

The longer you live
all the more time you have
to accomplish little acts of kindness

When we use our time here on Earth wisely
we will be amazed to find every thing counts

Where ever you find yourself now enjoy your life
making the time left one of joy and happiness

About the Author--Nancy S. Calumet

Nancy S. Calumet is the founder of Tri-Angel Ancestry, a family partnership founded in 1992 for teaching Reiki and sending Reiki to those in need. She is a certified Reiki Master Teacher and member of the Keweenaw Bay Indian Reservation L'Anse, Michigan. Her given spirit name is Morning Star Woman. Nancy is recognized for her professional skills and accomplishments acquired over 40 years in the nursing profession specializing in management, education and quality assurance. Widowed in 1990, it was through Reiki and writing poetry she found true emotional healing. Now retired, she resides in Springfield and welcomes your comments. Her email address is nancycalumetrn@gmail.com

The poem, Little Gems is reprinted by permission from Mrs. Calumet's book of poetry, GEMS, available on Amazon.com, and more.